The value of spiritual duty in Bhagavad-Gita and Taoism

Dr. Sanoo Tiwari

BlueRose ONE.com
Stories Matter
NewDelhi • London

BLUEROSE PUBLISHERS
India | U.K.

For permissions requests or inquiries regarding this publication, please contact:

BLUEROSE PUBLISHERS
www.BlueRoseONE.com
info@bluerosepublishers.com
+91 8882 898 898
+4407342408967

ISBN: 978-93-5704-694-7

Cover design: Tahira
Typesetting: Tanya Raj Upadhyay

First Edition: July 2024

Dedication

I humbly dedicate this work at the lotus feet of the Omniscient and Beneficent Almighty God and my dear parents without whose inspiration, guidance and blessings I could have never completed this work dealing with two gigantic ancient religious and spiritual traditions of the world.

Acknowledgement

The present work is the fruition of the guidance and blessings of many people who inspired and motivated me to study in detail the relevance, nature and significance of duty in a person's life, as also the role played by religion and spirituality in this context. More specifically, the value and significance of duty in a religious-spiritual framework had always intrigued me in the context of numerous anecdotes belonging to different religious and spiritual traditions illustrating incredible commitment to one's duty even in the face of fatal challenges. I had always wished that my academic pursuit should serve positively the life and thoughts of common people. I believe this work would certainly fulfil this wish of mine.

The conceptual framework of this work had taken shape through the course of my Doctoral research in the Department of Philosophy and Religion, Banaras Hindu University, as this work is largely based on that research. Therefore, it is my duty to first of all express my gratitude to Banaras Hindu University and more specifically to the Department of Philosophy and Religion for giving me the valuable opportunity to pursue this study in detail. Also, I would take this opportunity to express my thankfulness to the University Grants Commission for supporting me financially through its fellowships during the course of my research.

Next, I would like to express my deep gratitude to Prof. R. K. Jha, my Research Supervisor, for guiding me effectively through the course of my research. Without his inspiration, motivation and guidance this academic project could not have achieved the shape it has. In addition to my Supervisor, many senior faculties of the Department too had helped me with their positive feedbacks which surely contributed to enhancing the quality of my study. In this connection I would like to thank Prof. M. R. Mehta, Prof. S. P. Pandey, Prof. Ananda Mishra, Prof. Sachchidananda Mishra and Prof. S. C. Dubey for their kind words of wisdom and motivation.

I also take this opportunity to acknowledge my eternal indebtedness to my dear parents without whose support and encouragement I could not have even imagined to complete a task of this proportion. I always look forward to their blessings and support in all my endeavours.

Last but not the least, I bow my head before the Almighty Divine Shakti whose wish and blessings are the primary cause for the manifestation of anything worthwhile in this creation. Without Her blessings and compassion even the mightiest cannot move even a blade of grass, as narrated in the Kena Upaniṣad.

Foreword

The book entitled "Value of Spiritual Duty in Bhagavad-Gita and Taoism" by Dr. Sanoo Tiwari is a critical, comprehensive and comparative study of spiritual duty in two different glorious traditions: Bhagavad-Gita of India and Taoism of China. There are many writings on duty in Bhagavad-Gita and Taoism; however, the distinctiveness of this book is that it is not only a comparative study of duty explained in Bhagavad-Gita and Taoism but also sets down the metaphysical foundations of spiritual duty.

In this book, Dr. Tiwari focuses on two things: firstly, spiritual duty and secondly, the metaphysical ground of spiritual duty in Bhagavad-Gita and Taoism. Spiritual duty is different from the performance of religious rituals. Although the terms spirituality and religion have always been used in the same sense, however, close in-depth study of these two concepts spell out that there are nuance differences between them. The term religion has been used especially for Semitic or Prophetic or Missionary or Institutional or Organized religions, which are principally three: Judaism, Christianity, and Islam. Certain features of religion differentiate it from spirituality, for example, the concept of the prophet, a unique scripture, a particular kind of ritual, the feeling of religious organization, and eventually, the faith. It is pertinent to mention that ritual parts are very much dominant in religion. Spiritualism crosses the boundary of rituals, and it focuses on self-realization. Spiritualism, therefore, means self-realization or abidance in the soul.

Spirituality and religion can beautifully be delineated by the example of a circle. A circle has three significant components: Centre, Radius, and Circumference. Here, the Centre represents the self; the Radius represents the mind, whereas the Circumference represents the physical body. If one increases the length of the radius, i.e., mind, naturally, he/she goes far from the center, i.e., self. Since religion mainly emphasizes rituals, it goes far from the center, i.e., self-realization. However, if one diminishes the radius length, he gradually comes closer to the center, i.e., the self, which is the essence of spirituality. Thus, the initial point of both spirituality and religion is the same; however, their ends are different from each other. One is focused on self-realization, whereas the other is satisfied with the performance of a stereotype of ritual and never wants to cross its boundary.

This book accentuates the value of spiritual duty and endeavours to discover its metaphysical ground. Naturally, duty is an essential part of our life. Performance of duty, however, may be independent of the ontological ground (one can see its best example in Kant's philosophy, which is known as deontological ethics), or it may be underpinned on the ontological ground. Let us suppose that it has no ontological foundation, in that case, it can neither explain "the eternity of spiritual values" nor it can give a satisfactory answer to this question: "Why should one be moral at all times?" This question can be satisfactorily answered in the light of metaphysical exposition.

The main objective of this book is to elaborate the doctrine of *Anasakta Karma*, i.e., the performance of duty with complete devotion without any interest or with complete detachment. It is known as "the state of inaction in action". "Inaction in action" is not the denial 'of action,' but the denial of 'in action.' It is the composition of two things: action as well as renunciation. By virtue of this, Bhagavad-Gita reconciles both opposite ways of action: 'way of action' and 'way of renunciation.' More or less, the same mode of action has also been accepted in Taoism. There is the concept of *'wei-wu-wei'* in Taoism, which means 'action in non-action'. On the one hand, it denies worldly desire-based actions; on the other hand, it also substantiates those actions concerning the wellness of all beings without any self-interest. Apart from this, both thoughts believe in the supreme or ultimate reality and elucidate duty in the light of metaphysical ground. If duty is bound up with ultimate truth, it becomes spiritual duty.

In this book, Dr. Sanoo Tiwari opens up a new dimension in understanding the spiritual duty, particularly in the context of Bhagavad-Gita and Taoism. It is a valuable resource for the lovers of Bhagavad-Gita and Taoism in general and metaphysical exposition of spiritual duty in particular, offering fresh insights that will inspire a new generation to comprehend these profound thoughts in a different perspective. I congratulate Dr. Sanoo Tiwari for her exceptional work and wish her every success in her future endeavours.

Rishi Kant Pandey
Professor & Head
Department of Philosophy
Allahabad University

Preface

The present volume seeks to discuss the concept of spiritual duty in the context of Bhagavadgītā and Taoism. Whereas Bhagavadgītā represents the essence of the Vedic tradition and illustrates the core of spirituality permeating the Indian subcontinent, Taoism represents a major religious and spiritual tradition permeating the vast Chinese territory. Thus, they are representing two major ancient spiritual traditions of the world. Now, the concept of duty is inalienable to our personal and social life since the time of earliest human civilizations. Perhaps, it is the concept of duty that primarily distinguishes human life from animal life. Animal life is believed to be mostly guided and controlled by natural instincts which means there is an absence of an explicit sense of 'ought' in animal deliberations. On the other hand, human life is apparently obsessed with the sense of 'ought' in all of its activities. Humans are never satisfied with any instinctive explanation for their activities. Any such instinctive justification is clearly deemed insufficient and derogatory. Thus, the dominance of this 'ought' sense is the distinguishing characteristic of human life and its psychological framework.

This 'ought' sense in intertwined with the concept of duty since duty is primarily understood as what one ought to do. Duty is a normative reference point for human activities. However, such a normative reference point cannot hang in isolation, aloof from the other aspects of human understanding and behaviour. Almost all aspects of human understanding, behaviour, psycho-physiological constitution and cultural framework influence the unique flavour of 'ought' and duty relevant for a person and community. Holistically speaking, the complete worldview entertained by a person goes a long way in shaping the sense of duty relevant for that person.

Broadly speaking, there are two prominent worldviews noticeable through the course of development of human civilization viz. the materialist and the spiritualist worldviews. Of course, it must also be conceded upfront that within the fold of any of these alternative worldviews all individuals will certainly have their own unique shades of the conception of duty relevant for them. On the other hand, it may also be submitted that certain broad features may be noticeable as commonly characterising all the individual understandings of duty falling within any given alternative worldview. In order to briefly note the prominent materialist conceptions of duty many western ethical theories have been discussed. On the other hand, in order to understand the spiritualist conceptions of duty two major ancient spiritual traditions have been taken up for discussion.

As pointed out earlier, the entire worldview entertained by a person becomes relevant to one's formulation of the notion of duty. Therefore, before discussing the notion of duty in the spiritualist framework of Bhagavadgītā and Taoism, separate chapters have been devoted to the discussion of the cosmic metaphysical frameworks entertained by these spiritual traditions. Following that, the unique characteristic notions of duty enunciated by these spiritual traditions have been discussed in order to highlight their chief characteristics and merits, as also their linkages with their respective metaphysical frameworks.

In the context of Bhagavadgītā, the concept of Niṣkāma-karma emerges as the most relevant candidate for the representation of spiritual duty in the context of its metaphysical framework. Roughly speaking, Niṣkāma-karma stands for actions characterised by an absence of all forms of attachment on the part of the agent to the envisaged goals and objectives of that action. That is, Niṣkāma-karma requires that the agent of action must be free of all selfish attachments and aversions and instead should be guided primarily by the deepest metaphysical nature of the Self or Ātman. The metaphysical framework of the Bhagavadgītā presents a unique viewpoint for understanding the world and oneself and this very viewpoint is to be made the guiding light for developing the sense of 'ought' and duty relevant to one's activities. The spiritual nature of the Ātman and the world lying at the root of one's notion of duty is sufficient to proclaim Niṣkāma-karma as the spiritual duty advocated in the framework of the Bhagavadgītā.

The metaphysical framework of Taoism too emerges explicitly spiritual when one takes into account its description of the nature of Tao. Taoism advocates going with the flow of nature and carefully shunning all artificial behaviours. It values emptiness where emptiness stands for making oneself devoid of all selfish thoughts and motivations. The other facet of this emptiness is spontaneity. Such spontaneity is rooted in the nature of the Self as being identical with the Tao. All these conceptions jointly lead to the formulation of the Taoist notion of Wei-Wu-Wei, which literally means 'action-in-inaction'. Wei-Wu-Wei stands for actions characterised by emptiness i.e. absence of all selfish and artificial motivations behind an action. When such emptiness is realized all actions become spontaneous, springing from the innermost nature of the Self as being identical with the Tao. Thus, for Taoism the greatest ought and spiritual duty consists in refraining from all selfishness and artificiality; thereby facilitating one's stabilisation in the nature of Tao. Once such stabilisation in the nature of Tao has been realized, each and every action of that person becomes a spontaneous manifestation of the wish of Tao and so it can never be imperfect or misdirected.

With reference to the above mentioned two important illustrations of spiritual duties, a comparison is made with the representative materialist notions of duty and their merits and demerits have been pointed out. It is noted at this point that the worldviews nurtured by the materialist and spiritualist frameworks have far reaching influences on the notion of duty developed in those frameworks. While the morality of the materialist duty involves a great amount of effort and deliberation, the morality of the spiritual duty reveals itself as natural and effortless. This also reveals the fallible and fluid nature of the materialist sense of duty which is contrasted with an almost infallible and solid nature of the spiritual sense of duty.

In the contemporary scenario where people in general are turning more and more suspicious and hostile towards the relevance and utility of spiritual traditions, I have sought to make a humble contribution towards establishing and highlighting their unique characteristics and superiority, specifically with reference to the notion of duty, which lies at the core of our lives and gives desirable or undesirable forms to our lives and surrounding circumstances. I hope this work makes a positive difference to our lives and understanding.

Table of Contents

Chapter 1: What is Duty?

Ethics primarily deals with the concept of duty and duties are essentially understood in terms of prescribed and prohibited actions. Actions constitute the very essence of human life since life progresses and takes shape in accordance with our actions. Duty is concerned with the 'ought' nature of actions. It is a normative concept. Therefore, it is very difficult to decide which actions should carry the 'ought' tag. Ethics, being the study of morality and normative issues, is directly concerned with the nature and determining criteria of duties. According to the choice of the criteria which determine our duties, different ethical theories of duties take shape.

This book aims to study the concept of duty with reference to two great spiritual traditions, namely the Indian tradition of Bhagavadgītā and the great Chinese tradition of Taoism. However, before starting the discussion it would be relevant to present an outline of the various important theories of duty. However, this introductory discussion is not intended to be exhaustive. In this context, some of the important theories shall be taken up and the nature of duty explicitly discussed there or implied there will be highlighted, so that the varieties in the conceptions come out clear. This is important for highlighting the points of similarities and dissimilarities obtaining between the ethical theory of duty and the spiritual tradition-based conception of duty. The objective of the book is to find out if there is something different in the conception of duty with reference to these two spiritual traditions vis-a-vis the usual philosophical theories of duty. It would also be interesting to examine if there are any inherent advantages or disadvantages associated with the spiritual notions of duty.

Before starting with the specific discussions of various ethical theories about duty, it is important to be clear on some of the basic concepts in this field. The concept of ethics, morality and values are important in this connection. Ethics can be understood as the philosophical and higher-level study of morality and values in their various aspects. On the other hand, morality stands for the prevailing and accepted cultural norms of behaviour in any given space and time. It provides the norms for distinguishing between good and bad, or desirable and undesirable. Morality tells us what kinds of thought, speech and action should be considered good and what should be considered bad. Morality is greatly influenced by cultural and historical factors. Therefore, one should always talk about morality with reference to the community in question and the historical time period to which it belongs. In contrast, values refer to the criteria which are used for distinguishing between the good and bad, the right and wrong. Whichever thought, speech and action supports or enhances a given value, is considered good. The thoughts, speeches or actions that oppose or diminish a value, are considered bad. So, values are critical for deciding the goodness and badness of any thought, speech or action.

Values serve as the objective that are sought to be realised through the performance of moral acts. Values can be of two kinds - intrinsic and extrinsic or instrumental. Intrinsic values are such values which are sought to be realised for their own sake. They are the ends in themselves. However, instrumental values are those values which facilitate one's moving closer to some intrinsic value. That is, instrumental values are considered values because they facilitate the realisation of some intrinsic value.

1.1 Duty in Aristotelian Ethics

In Aristotelian ethics the discussion of moral virtue occupies the central theme in the famous work, Nicomachean Ethics. The first important thing that Aristotle points out is that there are two kinds of virtues - intellectual and moral. Intellectual virtue is cultivated by learning it from the qualified teacher, whereas moral virtue has to be cultivated by practising it. Only by practising moral virtues, it is possible for a person to become virtuous.[1] For example, only by performing just acts and brave acts repeatedly, does one become a just or a brave person. It is the nature of the repetitive performance that determines the quality and intensity of the virtue in a person. Therefore, Aristotle believes that virtue comes from habit. One cannot first learn virtue and then act virtuously. Instead, *it is by acting virtuously that one becomes virtuous.* That is why Aristotle says *"Thus, in one word, states of character arise out of like activities. This is why the activities we exhibit must be of a certain kind; it is because the states of character correspond to the differences between these. It makes no small difference, then, whether we form habits of one kind or of another from our very youth; it makes a very great difference, or rather all the difference."*[2] Aristotle considers happiness to be the ultimate end of all endeavours but happiness cannot be considered as a passive disposition, since otherwise it would have been available to even the life of the plant. Happiness consists in some activity and while some activities are required for the

[1] Singer, Peter, *Ethics,* 1994, pp. 26-7.

[2] Aristotle, *Nicomachean Ethics,* pp. 28-9, as cited in Singer, 1994.

sake of something else, other activities may be considered necessary and desirable in themselves. Out of these two classes of activities, happiness clearly belongs to the class which is an end in itself. It must be so because happiness is self-sufficient, from which nothing else is sought besides that activity. The activities related to virtuous actions also belong to the same class and lead to happiness.[3]

The disposition of each person decides which kind of activity will be most desirable to that person. So, the nature of pleasant activities varies according to the disposition of that person. Now the disposition of a good man is considered virtuous. Therefore, the activity pleasant for the good man must be virtuous activity, providing him the happiness which is an ultimate end in itself. Relaxation and amusement cannot be considered happiness of that kind because it is not an end in itself. It provides relaxation, which then provides the necessary energy to him for engaging in his desirable activity. Happiness consists in virtuous activity and virtuous activities require exertion. Therefore, happiness cannot be equated with amusement.

If happiness consists in virtuous activity, it will follow that the highest happiness must be corresponding to the activity related with the highest virtue and further, that highest virtue must be related with that faculty of our being which is the best in us. According to Aristotle, the highest faculty in our being is that of reason and therefore rational contemplation is that virtuous activity which can be described as producing the highest happiness. This contemplative activity must be considered the best not only because reason is our best and unique faculty, but also because rational knowable objects are

---

[3] Singer, 1994, p. 185.

the best of all objects. Further this activity must be the best as it can be done more continuously than anything else. Its purity and enduring nature, as well as its self-sufficiency, definitely show the supremely happy nature of contemplative activity. This philosophical or contemplative reflection is most self-sufficient and is loved for its own sake. Therefore, such happiness describes the complete happiness of man. As far as a person engages in contemplative activity in accordance with his faculty of reason, to that extant he becomes successful in realising the highest happiness of man. Therefore, we must strive to the best of our ability to live in accordance with the faculty which is best in us, because the quality and worth of activity related with that faculty would far surpass the activities related with any other faculty. Therefore, it would be strange if a person were to choose not the life of his self but that of something else. For Aristotle, *"........ that which is proper to each thing is by nature best and most pleasant for each thing; for man, therefore, the life according to reason is best and pleasantest, since reason is more than anything else is man. This life therefore is also the happiest."* [4] This state of highest happiness is what Aristotle terms ***'Eudaimonia.'*** Striving for the realisation of eudaimonia is the highest duty in the view of Aristotle.

1.2 Duty in Deontological Theory

The deontological view of duty is one of the most prominent ethical theories of duty. This theory does not seek to derive the oughtness of duty from any divine source or even human cultures. It does not even try to relate oughtness of duty with the outcomes of moral actions. This theory seeks to discover the element of necessity and a-priori in the oughtness

[4] Aristotle, *Nicomachean Ethics*, as cited in Singer, 1994, p. 188.

of duty. That is why the deontological theories of duty are often referred to as ***'duty for duty's sake.'*** The traditional deontological theory of duty was given by Kant which shall be presently discussed. However, in recent times, other versions of the deontological theories of duty are also being discussed and they cannot be completely ignored.

1.2.1 Duty in Kantian Deontology

Kant begins his discussion of duty by pointing out that morality consists of categorical imperatives. A categorical imperative is contrasted with a hypothetical imperative. That is, a hypothetical imperative is a conditional command like - *if you wish to be healthy, then exercise regularly*. In contrast, a moral imperative is always a categorical imperative, according to Kant, which is not at all affected by the objective conditions or the subjective preferences. It is an unconditional command – *"....for a moral imperative holds unconditionally or categorically. This means that a moral imperative commands obedience for the sake of no other end than its own rightness."*[5]

Kant believes that the categorical imperative must be based in reason alone. Faculties other than reason are subject to various personal biases. Therefore, if the categorical imperative must have an unconditional oughtness associated with it, then that can come only from reason. Kant presents this basic rationality-based idea as a maxim which says *"Act only according to that maxim by which you can at the same time will that*

[5] Moore, Noel Brooke, and Kenneth Bruder, *Philosophy: The Power of Ideas*, Mayfield Publishing
Company, California, 1996, p. 232.

it should become a universal law."[6] That is, a maxim can be a moral principle only if it is universalizable. For example, if someone wishes to act on the maxim- *I shall make a promise now, but will not honour it later;* then if everyone were to act on this maxim, the act of promise itself would lose all meaning and in such a situation even the first person would not be able to act fruitfully on that maxim. This means the maxim itself cannot be universalized rationally. Therefore, it is unacceptable as a moral principle. The necessity of its non-universalizability flows from reason itself. Therefore, the oughtness of a moral principle is a matter grounded in reason alone. This also means that moral acts should be performed only out of a sense of rightness attached to them and deriving from reason. All other considerations are extraneous to the nature of the moral act. This is why in view of Kant, moral duty should be performed only out of a sense of duty and nothing else. This is also the reason that Kant's deontological theory is also known as *'the theory of duty for duty's sake.'*

Kant also pointed out that one should have the will to act on a moral maxim. However, no one can have control over the actual results flowing from that moral act, as various circumstances have the capacity to influence it. In such a situation, the goodness associated with the moral act can never be in terms of external situations or results or even internal dispositions. In Kant's view, the goodness associated with the moral act is purely in terms of the will to act on the moral maxim, just for the sake of its being a moral duty. Kant says "Nothing can possibly be conceived in the world, or even out

---

[6] Kant, Immanuel, *The Foundations of the Metaphysics of Morals,* as cited in Singer, 1994, p. 274.

of it, which can be called good, without qualification, except a goodwill."[7]

In the discussion of Kantian duty, reason has a place of paramount importance. It is so because he explains the principle of morality as deriving purely from reason alone. This outlook leads to another important aspect of Kant's theory of duty. Since all human beings are uniquely and necessarily rational, therefore no moral maxim should be allowed to treat any human being as inferior or superior in the context of their reasoning faculty. That is to say, treating any human being as inferior must be treated as an immoral act. This necessary implication has been stated by Kant as the practical imperative, which says, *"Act so that you treat humanity, whether in your own person or in that of another, always as an end and never as a means only."*[8]

This way, Kant has discussed the concept of duty in the deontological framework, where he derives the necessity of acting morally purely on the basis of reason. The willingness of a person to act out of such necessity is the only kind of will that can be treated as an unconditional goodwill. In the view of Kant, acting morally has nothing to do with human virtues, philanthropy or even divine dictates. His treatment of morality and duty was path breaking and presents an entirely new framework for understanding duty and morality.

1.2.2. Duty in Contemporary Deontology

The deontological theory of duty has been contrasted with the teleological theory in contemporary period to highlight the

[7] Moore and Bruder, *Philosophy: The Power of Ideas*, 1996, p. 232.

[8] Kant, Immanuel, *The Foundations of the Metaphysics of Morals*, as cited in Singer, 1994, p. 279.

distinct uniqueness of the deontological view of duty. The word 'deontological' derives from the Greek term *'deon'* which means duty, whereas the word 'teleological' derives from the Greek term *'telos'* which means goal. The basic idea of deontological theory of duty is that some acts are by their very nature unacceptable and wrong and hence they ought to be morally prohibited. There is no further criterion with reference to which the wrongness of those acts needs to be established. Therefore, usually the deontological theory of duty gives prohibitions as morally obligatory and positive prescriptions are generally understood indirectly. However, the stress of the deontological theory clearly lies on prohibitions. As Fried says *"it is part of the idea that lying or murder are wrong, not just bad, that these are things you must not do - no matter what. They are not mere negatives that enter into a calculus to be outweighed by the good you might do or the greater harm you might avoid. Thus, the norms which express deontological judgements - for example, 'Do not commit murder' - may be said to be absolute. They do not say: 'Avoid lying, other things being equal', but 'Do not lie, period'."*[9]

In contrast, the teleological theory of duty seeks to determine the moral quality of an act with reference to its consequences. That is, the goodness of an act has to be understood by a comparative assessment of its consequences. Therefore, this approach of morality and duty is also known as *Consequentialism.* Fried and other contemporary deontologists have discussed their views by contrasting them with the consequentialist moral theories. One of the basic points of the deontological theory is their belief that right is not

---

[9] Fried, C., *Right and Wrong,* Harvard University Press, Cambridge, Mass., 1978, p. 7, as cited in

Singer, Peter, ed., *A Companion to Ethics,* Blackwell Publishers, Oxford, 1994.

to be defined in terms of the good. They do not accept the idea that the concept of good is logically prior to the concept of the right. They hold that there is no necessary linkage between the good and the right. Moreover, Fried clearly states *"...the goodness of the ultimate consequences does not guarantee the rightness of the actions which produced them. The two realms are not only distinct for the deontologist, but the right is prior to the good."*[10] The various negative prohibitions which are presented as morally obligatory, may be simply referred to as 'deontological constraints.' Such deontological constraints oblige us to refrain from committing the concerned acts even when their non-performance clearly results in lesser good or greater evil. This clearly brings out the fact that the deontological approach to duty is non-consequentialist as it does not try to maximise any moral quality or even does not try to comparatively evaluate the possible consequences.

The consequentialist theories based themselves on the impartial consideration of the welfare of others. In contrast the deontological theories do not base themselves on such impartial consideration. For example, when harming an innocent person is prohibited deontologically, then even harming one innocent person cannot be acceptable, even if the situation results in the harming of many other innocent persons. That is, the deontological view does not try to put together the welfare of many persons to evaluate the morality of the concerned action. In the deontological view, it is important to stick to the prohibitions, irrespective of the consequences. Further, the deontological view does not allow the violation of a deontological constraint even if it leads to a situation where many other persons may have to face the

---

[10] Ibid., p. 206

situation of violating the deontological constraint. This means sticking to and following the deontological constraints in our own capacity is of ultimate importance, irrespective of all possible consequences.

Many contemporary deontologists have criticised the consequentialist view on the ground that it leaves no room for personal autonomy. It presents a calculus for the maximization of welfare and goodness which leaves no room for personal choice and autonomy and this situation is not conducive for any moral framework. In contrast the deontological view clearly lays stress on the personal autonomy of the moral agent and his strict adherence to the deontological constraints. The deontological view clearly treats the virtue of the moral agent himself to be much more important than the virtues of other persons. Preserving our own moral virtue and sticking to deontological constraints is considered more important than the virtues of other persons or their following of the deontological constraints. This means personal autonomy and moral choices are clearly emphasised in the deontological view.[11]

There are three important features of deontological constraints in the view of contemporary deontologists. First, the deontological constraints are negatively formulated. For example, "Do not lie" is a deontological constraint, but this cannot be understood as "Tell the truth." Deontologists do not believe that the negative deontological constraints entail or are equivalent to their corresponding positive prescriptions. Thus, whatever remains outside the purview of the deontological constraint, is not taken to be morally obligatory. For example,

---

[11] Singer, Peter, ed. *A companion to ethics,* Blackwell publishers, oxford, 1994, p. 207.

the deontological constraint "Do not lie" does not oblige one to tell the truth.

The second feature of deontological constraints is that they are narrowly framed and bounded. They are precise in pointing out what has to be prohibited so that there may not be any confusion regarding it. The third feature of deontological constraints is that they are narrowly directed. That is, they are focused on the decisions, intentions and actions of the moral agents. They do not focus upon the entire range of possible consequences of the moral action. This point has been highlighted by Nagel - *"... deontological reasons have their full force against you're doing something - not just against its happening."*[12] The narrow directedness of the deontological constraints is directly related with the concept of moral agency and it is based in the distinction between intention and foresight. In the deontological view, a moral agent is responsible for only the things that he intends to do and not for all the unforeseen consequences of the moral act.

In the view of contemporary deontologists, the most important moral distinction lies between the permissible and the impermissible. Moral obligation or duty consists in not doing what is impermissible. Moral obligation is not in terms of the permissible. For the deontologists, an act may be permissible even though it may not be the best option or even a good option. On the other hand, for the consequentialist, an act can be morally permissible only if it is the best possible option for the maximization of moral goodness.

---

[12] Nagel, T., *The View from Nowhere,* Oxford University Press, New York, 1986, p. 177.

Another interesting point of contemporary deontological theory of duty is presented by the principle of double effect. Both Fried and Thomas Nagel approve of the traditional principle of double effect, which Nagel presents as *"...to violate deontological constraints one must maltreat someone else intentionally. The maltreatment must be something that one does or chooses, either as an* <u>*end*</u> *or as a means. The other than something one's actions merely cause or fail to prevent but that one doesn't aim at."*[13] That is, it is obvious that violating a deontological constraint means doing something wrong. However, even if such an action is done but there is no involvement of intention to do so, then the deontological view would not blame the person for any wrongdoing. That is, a moral agent would be blamed for doing something wrong only if there is the intention to do such an act. In this manner, the intention of the moral agent becomes a very important factor for deciding the moral credit or discredit of the agent.

1.3 Duty in Consequentialist Ethics

Any moral theory deals with the concept of ought and tries to understand the various aspects of what ought to be done. Any moral theory involves two important aspects. First, it involves some form of the theory of good or what is valuable. Secondly, it also involves the concept of the right. Different moral theories present different understandings of the concept of good or valuable, depending on the nature of their theories; but what is common to all the different presentations of the concept of good is that the good or valuable cannot be something which is essentially related to a particular

[13] Nagel, T., *The View From Nowhere,* Oxford University Press, New York, 1986, p. 179.

individual or individuals. The good or valuable must be something which is possibly universal in nature and therefore can be associated with any individual or institutional agent.

The moral theory of the good deals with what is the concept of good or valuable or what should be considered the good or valuable. For example, some theorists may take the perfection of our potential virtues itself as the highest good. Some may take the realisation of our rational capacities as the ultimate good. Some may take the realisation of perfect harmony with the natural order to be the highest good. Similarly, there can be many other conceptions of the good. The other component of the moral theory is the concept of the right. The concept of the right in the moral context deals with what should be the way in which we respond to what is considered good or valuable. That is, how should an individual or institutional agent act so that the valuable and good may be realised in the best possible manner. So, the theory of right primarily deals with the different ways of acting in relationship with the concept of the good. On this criterion, there may be two kinds of responses and moral theories. They may be the called the consequentialist and non-consequentialist moral theories. In traditional terminology, they are also called the teleological and the non-teleological moral theories. The non-teleological moral theories are also commonly known as the deontological moral theories. Therefore, consequentialism is the moral theory dealing with the concept of the right or the appropriate manner of acting with respect to a given concept of the good.

Consequentialism points out that whatever values are considered good, they ought to be promoted by performing such actions which result in their promotion. That is, the promotion of the values is the proper response to the concept of the good or valuable. They also say that honouring those values may also be acceptable, but only as a means for the promotion of those values. Honouring them subjectively cannot be considered an end in itself. In contrast, the non-consequentialist approach points out that honouring and respecting the values and the good is an end in itself, so much so that even if such honouring ultimately results in the lesser promotion of those values, it will be acceptable to the non-consequentialists. In the framework of consequentialism, the individual and institutional agent and the good or valuable are considered to be in an instrumental relationship. That is, the moral agent, whether an individual or an institutional agent, is considered an instrument for the promotion of whatever may be considered the valuable properties. On the other hand, the non-consequentialists do not consider the values and the agents to be in any instrumental relationship. For them, the honouring of the values and the exemplification of those values in the self of the moral agent is itself the right way of responding to those values. It does not matter for them whether such exemplification of the values in the moral agent ultimately results in the lesser or greater promotion of those values in general.[14]

In order to explain the core structure of consequentialism two concepts are critical. First, there is the concept of an option and secondly, there is the concept of the prognosis related with an option. An option stands for any possible course of action that a moral agent may choose to realise. For example, an option may be represented by a proposition which is directly

---

[14] Pettit, Philip, *A Companion to Ethics,* ed. Singer, Peter, Blackwell Publishers, Oxford, 1994, p. 231.

behavioural such as 'I shall speak the truth' or it may be represented even by an indirect behavioural proposition 'I commit myself to the principle of truthfulness.' The important point regarding the concept of option is that the moral agent always has the possibility of choosing to realise it or not. Although an option is a possibility that the moral agent can choose to realise, the fact remains that even if it is realised by the moral agent, what shape that realisation will take ultimately in the real world is something that is not within the complete control of the moral agent. Whatever may be done by the moral agent by way of choosing and realising an option, the other individuals in the world and various other circumstances will also influence that option in various possible ways and this ultimately gives a shape to the final result of the realisation of that option. The final shape that the realisation of an option takes up, is what is called the prognosis related with that option. Therefore, the realisation of a single option by a moral agent can potentially lead to various possible prognoses. Consequentialism can be defined in terms of two propositions which are generally defended by its advocates – "*...every prognosis for an option, every way the world may be as the result of a choice of option, has a value that is determined , though perhaps not up to uniqueness, by the valuable properties realised there: determined by how far it is a happy world, a world in which liberty is respected, a world where nature thrives, and so on for different valuable properties; the value determined will not be unique, so far as the weightings between such properties are not uniquely fixed. 2- Every option, every possibility, which an agent can realise or not, has its value fixed by the value of its prognoses; its value is a function of the values of its different prognoses, a function* *of the values associated with the different ways it may lead the world to be."*[15]

1.3.1 Duty in Classical Utilitarian Ethics

Any theory of ethics consists of two important sections. One deals with the theory of good and the other one deals with the theory of right. There are two significant branches in ethics. One is the consequentialist approach and the other one is the deontological approach. Both these theories have an inherent reference to the concept of good. It is more explicit in the case of consequentialist theories where the ethical obligation is to promote the good as far as possible. On the other hand, in the case of deontological theories, there is an implicit involvement of the concept of good because the concept of duty is not value neutral. It involves a duty towards beneficiaries or benevolence and this idea of benevolence necessarily involves the concept of good. That is, even in the deontological approach, the concept of duty is somewhere or the other dependent on the concept of good. In this way the concept of good is the necessary component of all ethical theories.

The context of ethics is always society and social relations. The injunctions of ethics are always with reference to other people and the good that it may bring to the other people. More generally, it can be understood as injunctions which are relevant for enhancing the good of all sentient beings. This idea of a necessary reference to the good of others being involved in all ethical and moral injunctions, was amply highlighted by Henry Sidgwick when he questions whether anything can be really considered good if it does not make any

[15] Pettit, Philip, *A Companion to Ethics,* ed. Singer, Peter, Blackwell Publishers, Oxford, 1994, p. 232.

difference, direct or indirect to any being's state of consciousness. He has posed this question in his work *Methods of Ethics*. To put it in a more general manner, we can say that whenever a person may be faced with two goods where the former makes a difference to someone and the latter does not make a difference to anyone, then a common-sense morality would obviously prefer the former good. That is, the inherent sense of good is always with reference to the betterment that it may bring about in the state of consciousness of some being.

The great strength of utilitarianism lies in the fact that it is non-committal to any specific theory of the good. Utilitarianism, in general, covers a vast portion of the consequentialist framework and there are many seeds of utilitarian theories. Utilitarianism is emphatic on the point that utility for someone or a vast majority is the deciding criterion for deciding the goodness of a moral act. It is non-committal to the point as to which specific theory of goodness is accepted by the people. It is the interests and the preferences of the people which go to decide the utility of the moral act with reference to them. What theories of goodness are involved in the decision of those interests and preferences is not a direct concern of the utilitarianism. In this way, it is neutral to the various specific theories of goodness. That is why so many shades of utilitarianism have developed over time. But the most important point is that utilitarianism always points out that goodness must be decided in terms of the utility of moral act for someone or a vast majority. But what precisely is the meaning of utility. In general, utility is understood in the sense of usefulness. However, this meaning generates a further question - usefulness for whom and in what way. The answer to this question leads to the development of different shades of utilitarianism, among which we shall consider the highlights of classical utilitarianism and also some of the recent and contemporary developments in utilitarian theories. The tradition of classical utilitarianism starts with Jeremy Bentham. He proposes the concept of utility for understanding what should be the meaning of goodness. He says that utility consists in usefulness in promoting pleasure and minimising pain. This understanding of utility is clearly a hedonic or hedonistic conception of utility. Therefore, Bentham's utilitarianism is also often referred to as hedonic or hedonistic utilitarianism. However, this hedonic utilitarianism is grounded in a somewhat contingent hypothesis, which has a psychological nature. That hypothesis can be called psychological hedonism, which means any normal human being has a nature which desires the maximization of pleasure and the minimization of pain. However, it must be noted that the dependence of Bentham's hedonic utilitarianism on psychological hedonism is not a necessary characteristic of utilitarianism as such. Utilitarianism can retain its basic framework even though it may be devoid of its relation to psychological hedonism. The idea of what consists in the understanding of pleasure and pain for an individual goes a long way in determining the nature of utilitarianism. Therefore, different theories related to the conception of pleasure and pain lead to different versions of utilitarianism. Pleasure may not necessarily mean sensory pleasure. It can also mean intellectual pleasure or aesthetic pleasure or pleasure derived in charity or pleasure derived from sacrificing oneself for the sake of one's community or country etc. Therefore, utilitarianism presents a general framework for accommodating various possible theories related to different conceptions of pleasure and pain. [16]

Bentham's seminal work, *An Introduction to the Principles of Morals and Legislations,* was published in 1789. In the very beginning of this book, Bentham presents the principle of utility as follows *"nature has placed mankind under the governance of two sovereign masters, pain and pleasure. It is for that alone to point out what we ought to do...... By the principle of utility is meant that principle which approves or disapproves of every action whatsoever according to the tendency it appears to have to augment or diminish the happiness of the party whose interest is in question: what are the same things in other words, to promote or to oppose that happiness. I say of every action whatsoever, and therefore not only of every action of a private individual, but of every measure of government.* "[17]

In chapter 4 of this work Bentham presents a hedonic calculus for calculating the pleasures and pains generated by various actions. It mentions many factors which must be taken into consideration for properly assessing the quantity of the pleasure and pain. He points out that the intensity, duration, certainty or uncertainty and propinquity or remoteness of the pleasant and painful experience are critical factors for assessing its quantity. Moreover, the fecundity of the moral act for generating further pleasant or painful experiences must also be taken into account. And lastly, the number of persons who are affected by that action, also needs to be considered for the proper assessment of the pleasure or pain. All these

---

[16] Goodin, Robert E., Utility and the Good, *A Companion to Ethics,* ed. Singer, Peter, Blackwell Publishers, Oxford, 1994, p. 242.

[17] Bentham, Jeremy, *An Introduction to Morals and Legislation,* Dover Publication Inc., 2009, p. 1.

various factors together present the hedonic calculus of Jeremy Bentham.[18]

John Stuart Mill was a committed Benthamite. Just like Jeremy Bentham, he too was a hedonistic utilitarian. This means he accepted the fact that pleasure is the highest good. However, he identified pleasure with general wellbeing or happiness of the society at large. This leads to the concept of social utility. The objective of good actions and the result of good actions were considered for the promotion of this social utility. Up to this point, Mill largely agrees with the outlook of Bentham. However, on a different critical point, Mill clearly differs from the viewpoint of Bentham. Mill believes that just as in the consideration of various things, quality has to be considered along with quantity, similarly even in the case of considering pleasure or happiness, quality must be taken into account. He did not believe that pleasure should be considered only quantitatively and that there is no consideration of quality for pleasure. He held the clear opinion that intellectual pleasures are definitely superior to physical pleasures and he believed that a person who is aware of the nature of both kinds of pleasure, will definitely prefer to have intellectual pleasure rather than physical pleasure. Mill says in his book *Utilitarianism,* which was published in book form first of all in 1863, that *"It is better to be a human being dissatisfied, than a pig satisfied; better to be a Socrates dissatisfied, than a fool satisfied and if the fool, or the pig, are of a different opinion, it is because they only know their own side of the situation."*[19] Mill points out that a moral action which causes the promotion of general wellbeing

---

[18] https://en.m.wikipedia.org/wiki/utilitarianism

[19] Mill, John Stuart, ed. Crisp, Roger, *Utilitarianism*, 1998, Oxford University Press, pp. 56-57.

and happiness of the society or what can also be called social utility, is to be considered a good moral action. This means good moral actions lead to the promotion of social utility. This is not only a factual statement for Mill, but it is also a directive rule of moral conduct. He believes that everyone should desire to act morally in a manner that enhances social utility or the happiness of society. This objective is what Bentham had termed as the greatest happiness of the greatest number.

In his book *Utilitarianism,* Mill also discusses the proof that can be offered for his principle of utility. Before presenting his proof, he mentions that the proof that can be given for the visibility of an entity consists in only the fact that it is actually visible or the proof for the audibility of a sound consists only in the fact that it is actually audible and heard. Similarly, he goes on to argue that the fact of the desirability of utility cannot be doubted because everyone desires his own happiness. That is, happiness is desirable for each individual. From this it follows that happiness or utility can be desired and ought to be desired. In short, Mill argues for the desirability of happiness from the fact that it is actually desired by each individual. He treats this as a proof for the fact that utility is desirable, precisely because it is actually desired. He stretches this argument further and believes that since each individual desires his own happiness, therefore, all individuals taken together would desire the happiness of the entire community or society. That is to say, everyone taken together desires the happiness of the entire society. This means social utility is a desired and desirable end for the entire society.[20]

The proof given by Mill for his principle of utility has been widely criticised for involving various logical fallacies. Most

---

[20] https://en.m.wikipedia.org/wiki/utilitarianism

importantly, it has been charged with what is known as the naturalistic fallacy. In this fallacy one tries to deduce what one ought to do on the basis of what in fact he does. That is the normative aspect of an action is sought to be derived on the basis of a given fact. Another fallacy with which Mill's proof has been charged is the fallacy of equivocation. He has used the term desirable in two senses. One sense is that the thing in question is capable of being desired and the other sense of the term is that it ought to be desired. These two different senses of the word 'desirable' coming up in his proof are confused together and hence the fallacy of equivocation. The third fallacy involved is the fallacy of composition. Mill shows that because each individual desires his own happiness, therefore it can be deduced that all people together desire common happiness for the society. That is, from the fact of individual desires for one's own happiness, Mill deduces the position that everyone together desires the happiness of the society or social utility.

1.3.2 Duty in Contemporary Utilitarian Ethics

The discussion of utilitarianism in 20th century is significantly diverse from its discussion in the classical phase of Jeremy Bentham and J. S. Mill. Various theories have come up in contemporary times in connection with utilitarianism. These different theories present varying conceptions of utility and hence also the related concept of the good. Nonetheless, all these theories come under the purview of utilitarianism, because they all believe that the promotion of utility is the ultimate objective of morality.

One version of contemporary utilitarianism is known as ideal utilitarianism, which is generally associated with G. E.

Moore. However, the earliest description of ideal utilitarianism was given by Hastings Rashdall in *The Theory of Good and Evil* (1907). Moore had discussed ideal utilitarianism in his book Ethics which was published in 1912. Moore rejected the clearly hedonistic conception of utilitarianism that was given by the classical utilitarianism. He believed that there are a range of values that should be maximised for the maximisation of utility. He argued that it is intuitively clear that pleasure cannot be the only measure of goodness. He said there are many other values in the world such as knowledge, beauty, love, friendliness, loyalty etc. which are intrinsically valuable. The intuitive clarity of their value is difficult to doubt. Therefore, a world in which all such extra-hedonistic values are absent and has a certain given quantity of hedonist pleasure, would have to be strictly at par with a world in which the same total quantity of pleasure is there but it also contains these extra-hedonistic values. However, it is intuitively clear that there cannot be any intrinsic motivation for preferring the former kind of world as against the latter. This shows that in addition to hedonistic pleasures, the values and pleasures of the non-hedonistic type must also be taken into consideration for assessing the utility present in the world. This conception of utility is what is presented in the theory of ideal utilitarianism.[21]

In the fifties and sixties of 20th century vigorous debates took place regarding the central role of rules in the context of utilitarianism. This lead to the binary conception of act-utilitarianism and rule-utilitarianism. Two theories of utilitarianism, namely act-utilitarianism and rule-utilitarianism have developed through discussions and

---

21 https://en.m.wikipedia.org/wiki/utilitarianism

criticism in the mid-20th century. Smart and McCloskey had initially used the terms 'extreme' and 'restricted' utilitarianism but later on all the concerned philosophers settle on the terms act-utilitarianism and rule-utilitarianism. The basic difference between act and rule utilitarianism is that in the case of act-utilitarianism, an action is considered right if it maximises the resulted utility, whereas in the case of rule-utilitarianism, a moral action is considered right if that action conforms to a rule that maximises utility. In short, act-utilitarianism focuses on the utility maximising capacity of the act, whereas rule-utilitarianism reposes its faith in the utility maximising tendency of a rule that has been considered and settled with that end in purpose. However, it must be conceded that rule-utilitarianism ultimately has to depend on or may even collapse into act-utilitarianism. It is so because in case of exceptional situations, the rule for maximising utility may not be able to handle the peculiar case appropriately. In that situation for dealing with the exceptional moral case, a sub-rule may have to be devised and attached to the main rule for appropriately handling that situation. This means the utility generating effect of that exceptional situation and its related moral act must be considered along with the general rule and this surely means that the rule-utilitarianism has to take the support of act-utilitarianism to handle the cases of exceptional situations and moral acts. Nonetheless, the distinction of act and rule utilitarianism is broad based and various types of particular theories of utilitarianism can be classified into either act-utilitarianism or rule-utilitarianism.[22]

R. M. Hare introduced the concept of two-level utilitarianism. He also accepts that rule-utilitarianism

---

[22] https://en.m.wikipedia.org/wiki/utilitarianism

generally collapses into act-utilitarianism, but he points out that such a collapse is usually the result of allowing the rules to be very specific. Therefore, he suggests that the rules should be more general because the general rules of morality are usually framed for the purpose of moral education and serving as a general guideline for most of the moral cases. In this context, he suggests that a distinction should be made between 'specific rule utilitarianism' and 'general rule utilitarianism.' These two forms of utilitarianism comprise of Hare's two-level utilitarianism. He points out that usually the general rule utilitarianism should be followed and is followed by the people and only in exceptional situations specific rule utilitarianism needs to be brought up for the proper evaluation of that exceptional situation. He says *"One ought to abide by the general principles whose general inculcation is for the best; harm is more likely to come, in actual moral situations, from questioning these rules than from sticking to them, unless the situations are very extraordinary; the results of sophisticated felicific calculations are not likely, human nature and human ignorance being what they are, to lead to the greatest utility."*[23]

Another important version of utilitarianism in the twentieth century has been *preference utilitarianism*. It was first of all presented by John Harsanyi in 1977 in the work *Morality and the Theory of Rational Behaviour*. However, later on, the theory of preference utilitarianism came to be more commonly associated with R. M. Hare, Peter Singer and Richard Brandt.[24] Preference utilitarianism replaces Bentham's hedonistic psychology with the concept of preference satisfaction. By preference satisfaction we mean the satisfaction of individual

[23] https://en.m.wikipedia.org/wiki/utilitarianism

[24] https://en.m.wikipedia.org/wiki/utilitarianism

preferences as far as possible and for as large a number of people as possible. It subsumes within its fold the hedonic psychology of classical utilitarianism. There is nothing in preference utilitarianism which specifically requires anything to be within the fold of preferences. It just generally points out that whatever may be the preferences of the individuals, the maximum satisfaction of those preferences itself consists of the maximisation of utility. So much so, that even when the preferences go against the normal hedonic choices, it must be considered appropriate for the satisfaction of those preferences and the maximisation of the related utility.[25] Harsanyi rejected classical utilitarianism since he believed that in considering pleasure as the ultimate ideal and goal, classical utilitarianism is over dependent on an outdated hedonistic psychology. Such a hedonistic psychology cannot be substantiated by an unbiased empirical observation around us. Similarly, Harsanyi rejects the case of ideal utilitarianism by pointing that by general empirical observations, it can be easily concluded that any mental state, which has a purely intrinsic worth, cannot be commonly seen as an ultimate goal and ideal. That is, any intrinsically valuable mental state is certainly not commonly taken as the highest goal of morality. In place of these approaches, Harsanyi points out *"Preference utilitarianism is the only form of utilitarianism consistent with the important philosophical principle of preference autonomy. By this I mean the principle that, in deciding what is good and what is bad for a given individual, the ultimate criterion can only be his own wants*

[25] Goodin, Robert E., Utility and the Good, in Singer, Peter, *A Companion to Ethics,* 1994, Blackwell Publishers, Oxford, p. 243.

and his own preferences."[26] While discussing preference utilitarianism, Harsanyi adds two caveats. He distinguishes between the manifest preferences and the true preferences of people. Manifest preferences stand for those preferences which are clearly visible in the case of different individuals. On the other hand, true preferences represent those preferences that individuals would have if they had complete factual information regarding the issue at hand, perfect logical thinking capacity and freedom from all biases and unnecessary emotions. In this special situation, the preferences exhibited by an individual would be termed true preferences. It is with respect to such true preferences that Harsanyi talks of preference utilitarianism. The second caveat is that Harsanyi intends to exclude anti-social preferences such as enmity, jealousy, ill will, sadism etc. Individuals having such anti-social preferences cannot be considered bonafide members of a moral community. Hence, Harsanyi believes such anti-social aspects of individuals necessitate their exclusion from the moral community and therefore the preferences of such individuals cannot be considered seriously in the discussion of preference utilitarianism.[27]

Another very significant school of contemporary utilitarianism is *welfare utilitarianism.* It takes further the arguments presented in the two caveats of Harsanyi in his discussion of preference utilitarianism. Welfare utilitarians distinguish between preference-based standards of utility and interest-based standards of utility. They point out that it is very rare that an individual is having perfect factual

---

26 Harsanyi, John C., *Morality and the Theory of Rational Behaviour,* in Sen, Amartya; Williams Bernard, *Utilitarianism and Beyond,* Cambridge University Press, Cambridge, pp. 39-62.

27 https://en.m.wikipedia.org/wiki/utilitarianism

information regarding the issues at hand and he also has perfect logical thinking capacity and he is also free from all sorts of biases. Therefore, it is logical to think that ordinarily the preferences exhibited by individuals would not be those which truly maximise the utility for the individual and the society. On the other hand, interest-based standards of utility refer to the situation where there is perfect factual information, logical thinking capacity and freedom from all sorts of unwanted emotions and biases. In that special situation alone, the true interests of the individual and the society can be identified and these interests would depict the true welfare of the individual and the society. Therefore, understanding utility in terms of true welfare is the better way of maximising utility for the individual and society. However, it would not be true to say that interest-based standards of utility are completely disconnected from the preference-based standards of utility. In fact, they are the more basic and generalised forms of utility derived from the preferences of individuals. But what are the welfare interests of the individuals and society in a more specific sense? It is said - *"The most credible characterisation depicts them as simply being abstracted from actual and possible preferences. Welfare interests consist just in that set of generalised resources that will be necessary for people to have, before pursuing any of the more particular preferences that they might happen to have. Health, money, shelter, sustenance and such like are all demonstrably welfare interests of this sort, useful resources whatever people's particular projects and plans."*[28] In this way, the welfare interests of individuals and society represent the basic conditions which should be ideally fulfilled before anyone can effectively pursue his peculiar individual interests and

---

[28] Goodin, Robert E., Utility and the Good, ed. Singer, Peter, *A Companion to Ethics,* Blackwell Publishers, Oxford, 1994, p. 244.

preferences. Such a concept of welfare utility is also very important for deciding public policies because they generally affect the basic and common interests of all individuals in a community. In this way, welfare utilitarianism is a very significant development in the field of utilitarianism.

1.4 Duty in Virtue Ethics

The concept of duty in virtue ethics has to be understood in the light of the concept of virtue, which is the central theme in the discussion of virtue ethics. Virtue is intrinsically related with character and there are numerous questions which arise in connection with a virtuous character. *"Although 'virtue' sounds antiquated (non-philosophers would use words such as 'integrity' or 'character') questions about personal character clearly occupy a central place in ethics. Such questions concern what a 'good person' would do in real life situations. Champions of virtue, while not necessarily rejecting utilitarianism or rights-based theories, believe that those traditions ignore those central features of ordinary moral life involving character."*[29] Virtue ethics is also known as *aretaic* ethics. The term 'aretaic' derives from the Greek term 'arete' which means excellence or virtue. Virtue ethics, therefore, can be traced back to the ancient Greek tradition. Virtue ethics, in general, highlights the significance of the virtues of the mind and character. There are three important Greek concepts which are important for understanding the basic nature of virtue ethics. They are *arete, phronesis* and *eudaimonia. 'Arete'* literally stands for excellence or virtue and it represents a character trait which has become a settled pattern of behaviour or a kind of settled habit. Moreover,

---

[29] Pence, Greg, Virtue Theory, in ed. Singer, Peter, *A Companion to Ethics*, Blackwell Publishers, Oxford, 1994, p. 249.

virtue is taken positively so that a virtuous person is considered a good human being. Virtue cannot be equated with isolated single actions. It represents a more lasting feature in the character of the virtuous person. The virtue present in the virtuous person is considered responsible for his good actions in various different situations. It is not the other way round that certain actions are responsible for the virtue of a person. *'Phronesis'* is translated as practical wisdom or moral wisdom. It is considered an acquired trait. The uniqueness of this trait is that it enables the person possessing it to understand and identify what needs to be done in any given situation. It does not restrict itself to mere theoretical understanding, but goes on to propel the virtuous person to act in a virtuous manner in the given situation. In this way, *phronesis* may be considered the external and active manifestation of the internal virtue present in the virtuous person. The third concept, *Eudaimonia,* is well elaborated in Aristotle's Nicomachean Ethics. The term 'eudaimonia' has been variously translated as wellbeing, happiness, blessedness and also as human flourishing. In the context of virtue ethics, the meaning of eudaimonia as human flourishing becomes more relevant. Eudaimonia is not a subjective concept for Aristotle. It represents an objective state which can be equated with a life that has been lived well by a person of virtues. In the framework of Aristotle's thoughts, living a life of virtue, most importantly, consists in exercising the characteristic human quality of reason. That means a life lived in accordance with reason and actions done in the light of reason signify the nature of a virtuous person. Although the concept of eudaimonia was first discussed by Aristotle, it now belongs to the tradition of virtue ethics in a general manner and it represents a life fulfilled due to the presence of virtues in a person. The concepts of virtue and eudaimonia are teleological. That is, virtue is a means for the fulfilment of the higher purpose of human life. Just as the sharpness of a knife is its virtue because the purpose of a knife is cutting, similarly whatever may be considered the ultimate purpose or *telos* of human life, the characteristic traits of a person which enable its fulfilment have to be considered as virtues. Therefore, a virtuous character has the purpose and goal of fulfilling the higher and ultimate purpose of human life. However, there is a divergence of views regarding the ultimate goal of human life and hence there is also divergence of views regarding the virtues which should be considered necessary for the fulfilment of that goal.[30]

The beginning of modern virtue ethics is characterised by the effort to distinguish it from the ethical viewpoints of utilitarianism and deontology, or consequentialism and deontology. Whereas both deontology and consequentialism focus on moral actions to understand the nature of moral duty, virtue ethics instead focuses on the character of the virtuous person. Virtue ethics believes that actions do not comprise the virtuous character of a person. On the other hand, the character of a virtuous person is directly responsible for giving shape to moral actions in a stable and continuous manner in varying situations throughout the life of that person. Therefore, the virtues in the character of a person are the true reasons for the right selection and implementation of morally appropriate actions in various situations.[31]

The revival of interest in virtue ethics took place in 1980s, but it was actually the result of the works of two philosophers

---

30 https://en.m.wikipedia.org/wiki/Virtue_ethics

31 https://www.iep.utm.edu/virtue/

- Elizabeth Anscombe and Alasdair MacIntyre. In 1958 Anscombe pointed out that the historical notions of morality, in terms of duties and obligations, which in turn derived from the notion of *ought,* had become outdated. She believed that the society and state in which such moral concepts could be taken seriously were no longer available in contemporary times. Therefore, the theories of traditional morality such as utilitarianism and deontology were no longer relevant. She went to the extent of saying that these traditional ethical approaches were actually becoming harmful because they tried to present moral virtues as ends in themselves, without having any reference to human needs and desires. In this way, she highlighted the importance of giving central importance to virtues in the discussion of ethics and morality.

The idea of Elizabeth Anscombe was carried further by Alasdair MacIntyre in his ethical analysis. He believed that the modern societies have not inherited any one single ethical tradition from the past. In fact, they have inherited fragments of conflicting ethical traditions which are used for justified various actions in different spheres of public and private lives. He clearly dislikes this disoriented moral picture of the society and tries to revive a neo-Aristotelian account of human good, which would based in a set of moral and intellectual virtues. He believed that the concept of virtue becomes significant only in some given moral tradition and society. It cannot stand isolated in a vacuum. Therefore, he emphasized the need for commonly inheriting some moral tradition which would help in identifying the virtues that would fulfil the ultimate purpose of human life. A virtuous character has to serve as a means for realizing eudaimonia.[32]

1.5 Duty in the Ethics of Rights

The concept of rights is one of the central themes in the discussion of ethics and morality. The conception of duty, with reference to the ethics of rights, is a very specialized topic which can be understood only after understanding the moral conception of rights. The concept of moral rights can be traced back to the ancient Greek period in which the Stoic philosophers wondered about the relativity of human moralities with reference to different geographical and historical contexts. They wondered whether there was a higher standard of morality which could be common to all humanity and may not be varying from case to case. This gave rise to the concept of a higher natural law in the moral field with reference to which particular human moralities may be adjudged and evaluated and may even be found to be lacking in some respects. This conception of natural law that was imagined to be common and accessible to all human beings logically led to the conception of natural rights. Natural rights were supposed to be belonging to all human beings per se.

Another historical element that contributed to the development of the modern concept of rights was the contribution of the Christian tradition which talked in terms of religious obligations, duties and rights which were considered independent of the moralities set by any community or state. It went to the extent of believing that such religious rights and

---

32 Pence, Greg, Virtue Theory, ed. Singer, Peter, *A Companion to Ethics*, Blackwell Publishers, Oxford, 1994, pp. 250-251.

obligations could even provide a natural justification to revolt against an oppressive regime.

However, in the modern period, it was the British philosopher John Locke who declared the sanctity of the rights to life, liberty and property. His statement of these rights being fundamental to human morality was a massive leap in the ethics of rights which paved the way for its later recognition and incorporation into general morality and statecraft. In 1776, the Americans included the rights to life and liberty in their declaration of independence but substituted the right to pursuit of happiness in place of the Lockean right to property. Later on, in 1789, the French national assembly issued a declaration of the rights of man and of the citizen, which asserted the rights of liberty and property but also added on the right to security and resistance to oppression. Contemporary declarations of rights throughout the world can be classified into two categories. One category would be that in which there is a legal sanction to enforce those rights if they are violated. The other category is that in which the rights are declared as ideal aspirations towards which the human race should strive. The European Convention for the protection of human rights and fundamental freedoms of 1950 is an example of the first kind which has the International Court to enforce those rights with the help of the states endorsing that convention. The United Nations Declaration of Human Rights of 1948 is an illustration of the second kind where the rights are presented as ideal human aspirations.[33]

While the earlier 18th century conception of rights was restrictive and negative in character, limiting the functions of

---

[33] Almond, Brenda, in Singer, Peter, ed. *A Companion to Ethics,* Blackwell Publishers, Oxford, 1994, pp. 259-260.

governments; the modern conception of rights added the new positive element by incorporating the component of rights to various welfare goods. For example, the rights of state subjects to health, education, livelihood etc. presented a situation in which the government must expand its sphere of activity to fulfil such welfare aspirations. Such positive elements of rights required the expansion of government activity and jurisdiction. Therefore, one can talk of two kinds of rights - the negative rights and the positive rights. The negative rights entail what cannot be done by the government with reference to its citizens, whereas the positive rights entail what ought to be done by the government to fulfil the positive rights of its citizens related to their welfare aspirations.

In the discussion of morality and ethics, there are many key terms such as good, right, wrong, obligation, duty etc. and it can be easily seen that none of these terms can be considered as an exact substitute term for rights. The conception of rights has its own unique connotation. Therefore, the discussion of rights in the moral context must be considered relevant and justified. We have already seen that rights can be understood as positive and negative rights. In addition to this classification, another way of classifying rights would be in terms of human rights, moral rights and legal rights. Human rights would represent such rights which are accessible to all human beings by virtue of just being human beings. The universally accepted human rights present an ideal case for its acceptance legal implementation at the global level. The United Nations charter of human rights is an illustration of exactly this. Legal rights refer to the rights which are accessible to the citizens of a state by virtue of the constitution and legal framework of that state and which are ensured by the state to its citizens even under challenging circumstances. It should be noted here that all legal rights may not be moral rights as well. However, many of them could be moral rights as well. The third kind of rights, namely moral rights, stands for such rights which *ought* to be belonging to human beings by virtue of being moral agents and they would also include the rights belonging to non-human beings. All kinds of moral rights need not have legal sanction. That is to say, all moral rights may not be legal rights as well.

The concept of rights, like many other ethical concepts such as duties, obligations, goodness etc., cannot be considered a material or tangible thing. Yet, different ethical thinkers have different approaches to understanding the nature of rights. Broadly speaking, there are three ways of understanding the nature of rights. Firstly, there are some ethical thinkers who treat rights as facts and therefore treat statements about rights or statement of rights as factual statements because they think they can be adjudged true or false. The second category of ethical thinkers considers that statements about rights are not statements about facts. Rather, it is a statement about taking an emotivist position regarding the concerned issue and there is an implied support and prescription about that particular emotivist position. In short, for them, statements of rights are basically emotivist statements. The third category of ethical thinkers, represented prominently by American philosopher Ronald Dworkin, thinks that statements about rights are neither ordinary facts nor exclusively emotivist stances. Rather, they treat statements related to rights as a kind of moral fact, which has its own status and objectivity in the moral context.[34]

---

[34] Almond, Brenda, in Singer, Peter, ed. *A Companion to Ethics,* Blackwell Publishers, Oxford, 1994, p. 262

Rights can also be understood in two other ways. Rights can be taken as positive rights and negative rights. Alternatively, rights may also be understood as active rights and passive rights. In the case of positive rights, one would have the right to act or behave in a particular manner in the specified context, whereas in the case of negative rights one would have the right not to act or behave in some specific manner in the given situation. So, the difference between positive and negative rights is basically in terms of having the right to choose between acting or not acting in a particular manner. In the case of active right, the concept of right empowers the subject to act oneself in a particular manner in the given context. On the other hand, a passive right specifies that the subject has the right to be dealt with in a specified manner by some other individual in the given context. That is, in the case of passive rights, a person having a right of this kind is entitled to a specific kind of treatment coming from some other person.

There are varieties of ways in which the concept of rights may be understood. Broadly speaking, the most important ways in which rights may be understood are in terms of claims, powers, liberties and immunities.[35] Out of these four senses of rights the most dominant sense is that of a claim and this sense is a correlate of the concept of duty. Nonetheless, each of these four conceptions of right involves some conception of duty as well. This can be made clear with the help of relevant examples. For example, when we talk of rights as claims, we can think of the right of a person lending money to be repaid that loan back from the borrower. Now, the lender

35 Almond, Brenda, in Singer, Peter, ed. *A Companion to Ethics,* Blackwell Publishers, Oxford, 1994, p. 262

has a right to the money, whereas the borrower has a corresponding duty to pay back that loan to the lender. Thus, the concepts of claim and duty are both inter-related and also related to the concept of right. When we consider rights as powers, the right of a person to make his will and distribute his property according to his wish, is a matter of right, but at the same time the inheritor also may have a right to his legal heritage. That means, the right of the will-maker also involves the duty to ensure a legally and morally justifiable will. In this manner, rights as power and its correlated duty are intimately related to the same subject. When rights are considered as special liberties, for example, when the state or law gives the liberty to its citizens to choose whether they would like to do some activity which may be personally burdensome or disturbing to their mental health, it becomes a matter of choice for the citizen to act or to refuse to act with reference to that particular activity. For example, the state usually gives the liberty to its citizens of choosing not to provide any evidence against their spouses in the court of law. Here, rights in the sense of liberty enjoins the correlated duty upon the legal and state functionaries not to force the concerned citizen to act in a particular manner regarding which he may have that liberty. In this case, the correlated duty lies with the other persons and institutions. The fourth sense of rights as immunities may be understood as the case where a person is provided the freedom to act in a particular way without fearing any undesirable consequences arising due to some other persons or institutions and related to his activity. For example, participating in a democratic trade union or in a democratic organisation should not lead to any sort of retributive actions from the employer or employing institution against the person participating in the union. That is, taking part in a representative union has a corresponding right to be immune from any retributive action coming from the employer or employing institution. This means, rights in the sense of immunity implies and ordains a duty on the part of another person or institution not to act against that person for his concerned activity.

In this way, we can see that even though rights may be understood in varieties of ways, there is always an underlying sense of duty implied in it, whether it belongs to the primary subject or to the other subjects and institutions. On the whole, the concept of duty in the ethics of rights is sometimes explicit and sometimes implicit, but it is certainly involved in it in one way or the other. Of course, it is not necessary that the subject having the rights will always be himself the subject required to carry out its correlated duty. The correlated duty may very well lie with some other subject or institution.

1.6 Duty in Contractarian Ethics

Contractarian ethics tries to understand the nature of our ethical obligations, especially our political obligations, in the light of a social contract theory. Before the enlightenment era it was believed that one should obey the political rulers because of their divine right and status to rule us. That is, we must consider our self as divinely obliged to obey our rulers. However, in the enlightenment era this basic presupposition started to be questioned because the idea had gained acceptance that all human beings are naturally equal and hence no one can innately have the right to rule over others. In this situation, there was a need to explain political rulership and the obligation of the masses to obey their political masters. The explanation given for this constitutes the core of classical contractarian ethics. It was proposed that in the pre political age there was a sort of contract between the would-be rulers and the society that the members of the society would give up the certain rights, privileges and freedom so that the would-be ruler may exercise control over the society in a manner that would ensure collective security and harmony. That is to say, it was presented as a give and take solution to ensure the security and betterment of the society by giving powers to the rulers for a just and moral governance. However, by the turn of 18th century this classical contractarian version came to be questioned in terms of its ultimate legitimacy. It was asked why should one feel under an obligation to obey the rulers even if it is accepted that at some historical point there was a contract worked out between the rulers and the masses. The question still remained why we should go on honouring that contract. The obvious answer would be that once we have given a promise and our word to the ruler for obeying them, we should stick to it and obey the rulers. But this solution only begs the questions because the question still remains why we should go on honouring our historical promise. If it is answered by way of pointing out that it is one of our natural obligations to keep our promises, then the question comes up about the nature and legitimacy of natural obligations. Therefore, classical contractarian ethics came to be fundamentally questioned by the 18th century and as a result of that, other models of contractarian ethics came into being. There are basically two forms of contemporary contractarian theories. Both of them agree on the point that all human beings are naturally equal. However, they differ on the nature of equality that obtains naturally between the human beings. One approach emphasises the equality of physical power with respect to all human beings and therefore proposes that a contract between human beings must turn out to be mutually advantageous, because the state and the ruler ensure a harmonious co-existence of the members of the society. This contemporary contractarian approach may be called the 'Hobbesian Contractarianism.' On the other hand, the second approach emphasises the moral equality of all human beings. That is to say, all human beings are believed to have equal moral significance and concern. Therefore, a social contract situation would be such that it takes care of the concerns of each and every individual. This means that this approach emphasises moral equality and impartiality. This approach may be called 'Kantian Contractarian.'[36]

Hobbesian contractarianism basically seeks to present morality as a case of mutual advantage. It is grounded in the presupposition that all human beings are naturally equal and this equality is primarily in terms of their physical strength. While one may be free in visualising a society where everyone is free to do whatever one likes to ensure one's maximum advantage, it would actually mean that everyone gets pitted against everyone else for maximising their individual advantages. Surely, this would lead to a chaotic and disharmonious situation. It is to avoid such a chaos that a mutually advantageous social contract is proposed to ensure the maximum possible mutual advantage and harmony. This also means there is nothing inherently right or wrong in the Hobbesian contractarian model. This means there are no moral values as such. Therefore, the Hobbesian contractarian model does not actually present an alternative moral framework, rather, it presents an alternative to the moral framework itself.

---

[36] Singer, Peter, ed. *A Companion to Ethics*, Blackwell Publishers, 1994, p. 188.

It seeks to give a justification for socio-political rights and duties, while completely rejecting the earlier concepts of divine rights and duties and its associated idea of inequality among human beings. In this way, Hobbesian contractarianism tries to show that a mutually advantageous social contract can be the best way of ensuring socio-political harmony and mutual interests. However, there is a big problem in its presupposition, which is regarding the basic equality of all human beings in terms of their strengths. We know very well that in any society all human beings do not have equal physical, intellectual and emotional and also financial strengths. Therefore, they are not really equal to begin with. Because of this, the bargaining power of the strong individuals will be much more than that of the weaker individuals and as a result, the emerging social contract will certainly turn out to be having a greater advantage for the stronger individuals. This situation of unequal distribution of rights and duties could even lead to the convention of slavery and the Hobbesian model would not be in position to declare it as wrong or undesirable. It would be so, because it would be presented as an outcome of the social contract. Therefore, to the extent that the Hobbesian presupposition of the basic equality of all human beings is compromised in a society, there would be a lacking of justice in the structure of society emerging from that social contract.

The second version of contemporary contractarian ethics is the Kantian contractarianism, which seeks to present the concept of morality in terms of impartiality. Unlike the Hobbesian contractarianism, which practically replaces the traditional framework of moral obligations with its social contract version, the Kantian contractarianism tries to develop a social contract-based model of moral obligations. That is to say, it aims to strengthen the moral framework through the concept of social contract. The basic presupposition of Kantian contractarianism is regarding the moral equality of all individual human beings. This means each and every individual must be considered equally important in the moral context. The concerns of each individual human being must be given equal importance. Only then moral equality for all can be ensured.

The most well-known exponent of Kantian contractarianism is John Rawls. He believes people are *'self-originating sources of valid claims'* - i.e. people matter from the moral point of view, not because they can harm or benefit others (as in Hobbesian theory), but because they are *'ends in themselves.'* [37] Rawls believes that a moral version of the social contract can emerge only when each individual's concerns are given equal importance in the moral context. Therefore, the factual reality of inequalities pertaining to physical strength, intelligence, financial strength and emotional sensitivity are sought to be compensated by the acceptance of moral equality for all individuals. Rawls talks of the *'veil of ignorance.'* The veil of ignorance is the concept that one should visualize oneself as being in the position of any other randomly selected individual in the society to understand the morality and worthiness of any common obligation or duty that may have to be adopted by society. That is to say, before accepting anything as a duty or obligation according to the social contract, one must try to visualize its acceptability by each and every person in the society. So far, it is clear that Rawls seeks to work out a justified social contract in the light of the moral

---

[37] Singer, Peter, ed. *A Companion to Ethics*, Blackwell Publishers, Oxford, 1994, p. 191.

equality of all individuals. However, the question still remains as to how should one person understand the justifiability of any given obligation or duty associated with the social contract. Can there be a criterion for deciding this worthiness? The only answer that seems possibly coming in the framework of Rawls is that the reference must be made to our inner sense of justice. Certainly, this is not an objective or factual criterion and hence there can be many objections and doubts about it. But the important point is that the Kantian contractarian theory and the theory of Rawls seek to compensate for the practically available inequalities among humans with the concept of moral equality. Each individual must be treated as an end in oneself. Only when the social contract is worked out from an 'original position of equality,' the resultant social contract may be treated as morally justifiable.

Therefore, duty in the contractarian models is presented as arising from the social contract worked out by the people of society in a free manner. In the case of Hobbesian contractarianism, the presupposition is about the physical, intellectual equalities of all human beings and the resulting social contract presents itself as an alternative to the traditional moral framework. On the other hand, the Kantian contractarianism, illustrated by Rawls presupposes the moral equality of all individuals and uses our inherent sense of justice as a reference point for working out the social contract and presents it as a morally justifiable for understanding socio-political rights and duties.

Chapter 2: Cosmic Framework of Bhagavadgītā

Bhagavadgītā represents the very essence of Vedic tradition and it is perhaps the most commonly venerated scripture of the tradition. Although it is known as an independent scripture but actually it is a section of Mahābhārata, and it consists of 700 stanzas depicting the dialogue between Dhrtarastra and Sanjay. This dialogue represents the communication taking place between Krishna and Arjuna in the battlefield of Kurukshetra. It stretches from chapter 23 to chapter 40 of the Bhīṣma Parva of Mahābhārata. As such, it is traditionally believed to be authored by Veda Vyāsa. It shows conformity with the Vedas and yet it moves ahead of the Vedic content by suggesting new ways of interpreting the metaphysical implications of the Upaniṣads. It also discusses the various possible paths to spiritual enlightenment and liberation. In some respects, it is even path breaking from the traditional religious framework. Let us now take a look at some of its important concepts.

2.1 Brahman and Īśvara

The concept of Brahman represents the ontological absolute of the Upaniṣads, which means it is the sole reality. Logically, it implies that everything must be treated as somehow grounded in that higher reality, namely Brahman. The term 'Brahman' grammatically derives from the root verb *'Bṛh'* which means to swell, to expand, to grow, to evolve.[38]

[38] Sharma, C. D., *A Critical Survey of Indian Philosophy*, 1991, p. 24.

Hence, Brahman is believed to be that highest reality which has the nature of growing and expanding. Brahman is said to have two aspects, according to the Upaniṣads. The transcendent aspect of Brahman has been variously referred to as the *nirguṇa, nirākāra, niṣkala* and *para- Brahman.* On the other hand, the immanent aspect of Brahman has been variously referred to as the *saguṇa, sākāra, sakala* and *apara Brahman.* The transcendent aspect of Brahman is absolutely beyond the reach of space, time, causality, language and reason. Hence, it has been negatively indicated as *'neti-neti'* (not-this, not-this) by the Upaniṣads.[39] Śaṅkara has interpreted this *'neti-neti'* as a double denial of both the subject and the object. That is, the transcendent Brahman is beyond the categorization of subject and object. That is why, he refers to it as *'advaita'*, that which is beyond duality.

In contrast to the transcendent aspect of Brahman, the immanent aspect of Brahman is amenable to the categories of space, time, causality, language and reason. It is that aspect of Brahman which acts as the creator, sustainer and destroyer of the cosmos. This saguṇa Brahman is also referred to as *Īśvara* or God. *Īśvara* is the master of *Māyā,* the inscrutable and inalienable power of Brahman. Just as heat is inalienable from fire, so is Māyā inalienable from Brahman. Brahman, as conditioned by Māyā, is what is called *Īśvara* or God.[40] This Māyā is responsible for projecting an appearance of duality, space, time and causality, even though truly speaking, there is no duality but only the transcendent Brahman. This *Īśvara* creates the cosmos and is immanent in it. It is the soul of the cosmos and permeates both the sentient and the insentient

---

[39] Ibid., p. 280.

[40] Ibid., p. 280.

components of the cosmos. *Īśvara* has also been referred to as *'sat-cit- ānanda.'* [41] Sat stands for pure, unconditioned and infinite existence; cit stands for pure, unconditioned and infinite consciousness, whereas ānanda stands for pure, unconditioned and infinite bliss. The experiences of existence, consciousness and bliss that we have in the world are nothing but extremely microscopic and distorted appearances of the existence, consciousness and bliss that characterizes *Īśvara.*

Now, let us take a look at some of the representative stanzas from the Bhagavadgītā which throw light on the nature of Brahman and Īśvara. Bhagavadgītā (2-17) clearly states that the endless reality should be taken as that alone by which the whole cosmos is permeated.[42] That is, that Brahman which is beyond origination and destruction, is immanent in the whole cosmos; yet, in its own nature, it is also the transcendent absolute. It must be so logically as well because Brahman being the ontological absolute, there can be no existence of any entity apart from Brahman. Being so, whatever seems to exist, must ultimately be grounded in Brahman, which leads to the permeation of the entire cosmos by that Brahman. As a result of such cosmic permeation, the spiritually realized person is even-minded towards all, seeing Brahman alone as manifesting through all entities. Such persons alone are the true 'Puṇḍita', as they are the knowers of Brahman.[43] Bhagavadgītā clearly points out that Brahman alone is beyond all corruption and destruction.[44] Hence, Brahman is also the only *'akṣara.'* Even though that Brahman is

---

[41] Ibid., p. 280.

[42] *avināśī tu tat-viddhi yena sarvam-idaṁ tatam.*

[43] Bhagavadgītā, 5-18.

[44] Ibid., 8-3.

undivided, yet it appears as though divided amongst the various entities of the cosmos.[45] That Brahman itself also acts as the creator, sustainer and destroyer of the universe. That is, even though in its transcendent nature it remains indivisible ontologically, yet in terms of apparent manifestation, it projects itself as the world of plurality. It does all this through its own power, namely Māyā. It is Light of all lights and completely beyond the realm of illusory projections of Māyā.[46] It is of the form of pure intuitive knowledge; it is that which is known through pure intuitive and non-dual knowledge. This Brahman, of the form of pure knowledge, also resides in the hearts of all beings.[47] Bhagavad-gītā (13-30) points out that the person who is convinced of the fact all the pluralistic entities of the world are ultimately grounded in the highest Brahman and the whole cosmos is nothing but an epistemic extension of that Brahman, becomes identified with Brahman.[48] That is to say, that person realizes one's incorruptible metaphysical identity with Brahman. That Brahman, being omnipresent, resides in each particle of the universe, whether sentient or insentient. Even though it is inherently pure consciousness, yet because of its own wish and power, namely Māyā, it does not manifest itself in its pristine nature everywhere. There are various degrees of the manifestation of its consciousness in the different entities of the world. Being basically transcendent and attribute less, that Brahman does not actually get tainted by the activities and experiences of the material body in which it appears to be residing.[49] Just as even though ether is present

---

[45] Ibid., 13-16.

[46] *jyotiṣāmapi taj-jyotis-tamasaḥ param-ucyate,* Bhagavadgītā, 13-17.

[47] *hṛdi sarvasya viṣṭhitam,* Bhagavadgītā, 13-17.

[48] *....brahma sampadyate tadā,* Bhagavadgītā, 13-30.

[49] *.... Śarīrastho'pi kaunteya na karoti na lipyate,* Bhagavadgītā, 13-31.

everywhere, yet it does not get tainted by the attributes of the various entities due to its extremely subtle nature, similarly *ātman,* i.e. the Brahman's pure consciousness as manifesting through the material body, does not get tainted by the activities and experiences of the body because of its extremely subtle nature.[50]

Īśvara refers to that aspect of Brahman which is instrumental in the creation, sustenance and destruction of the cosmos. It achieves all this through its own infinitely mysterious power, namely Māyā. Those who understand the basic metaphysical identity of Īśvara and Brahman as well as the fact that everything in the world is under the complete control of Īśvara, naturally develop affinity towards it and this ultimately leads to constant remembrance and surrender to Īśvara, along with the firm conviction about the immanence of Īśvara in the whole cosmos. This state of mind exhibits ultimate devotion to Īśvara or God. The persons who are associated with such pure devotion or *bhakti-yoga,* become immediately eligible for complete identity with Brahman i.e. the highest liberation.[51] Bhagavadgītā goes to great lengths in emphasizing the fact that Īśvara is in no way inferior or secondary to Brahman. They are two faces of the same coin. It says categorically that Īśvara is the locus of Brahman. It is the locus and support of that which is immortal, eternal, undecaying and absolute bliss.[52] Once a person attains liberation, there is coming back to the realm of relativity and spatio-temporal plurality. That is, once a person realizes one's identity with Brahman, there is no possibility of reverting back

---

50 *....sarvatrāvasthito dehe tathātmā nopalipyate,* Bhagavadgītā 13-32.

51 *....brahma-bhūyāya kalpate,* Bhagavadgītā, 14-26.

52 Bhagavadgītā, 14-27.

to the realm of phenomenal world.[53] Bhagavadgītā describes Īśvara as that aspect of the transcendent Brahman which is immanent in the whole world and thus permeates all entities. Permeating everything in this manner, Īśvara sustains the whole world from within in a very subtle manner.[54] Since this Īśvara is greater than both the material corruptible world as well as the *Jīvātman* or individual soul, therefore it has been referred to as the *Puruṣottama* or the highest one.[55]

Now, the person who has intuitive knowledge of the basic metaphysical identity of the Nirguṇa and Saguṇa Brahman, as well as the knowledge of the immanence of Īśvara in the world, technically becomes one with Brahman. Such a person exhibits certain spiritual qualities, which are the consequences of his spiritual realization. He remains ever blissful, free from all anxieties and desires. He remains even-minded towards all living beings due to his conviction about the cosmic immanence of Īśvara. Being qualified by all these characteristics, he easily attains the highest devotion, *Parā bhakti,* to Īśvara.[56] Attaining such esoteric devotion to Īśvara, he comes to know intuitively the exact nature of Īśvara and Brahman. Attaining such esoteric knowledge of Īśvara and Brahman, one merges in Brahman by attaining perfect identity with that transcendent Absolute.[57]

This immanent Īśvara, being present in the hearts of all beings, sustains and controls all the beings in the world through its divine mysterious power Māyā. Although the

---

[53] *....yad-gatvā na nivartante tad-dhāma paramaṁ mama,* Bhagavadgītā, 15-6.

[54] *...yo loka-trayam-āviśya bibharty-avyaya īśvaraḥ,* Bhagavadgītā, 15-17.

[55] *...ato'smi loke vede ca prathitaḥ puruṣottamaḥ,* Bhagavadgītā, 15-18.

[56] *...mad-bhaktiṁ labhate parām,* Bhagavadgītā, 18-54.

[57] *...tato māṁ tattvato jñātvā viśate tad-anantaram,* Bhagavadgītā, 18-55.

phenomenal beings feel as if they are the agents behind all decisions and actions, yet the truth is that it is the subtle presence of Īśvara in all of them that continuously controls them and makes them decide and act in accordance with the requirements of their karmas. Īśvara resides in every heart and controls all like a machine is controlled and operated by some intelligent operator.[58]

In the light of the above discussion, it can be easily seen that as far as the Bhagavadgītā is concerned, it does not make a rigid distinction between Brahman and Īśvara. Of course, it does mention the two aspects of Brahman- Nirguṇa and Saguṇa, i.e. Para and Apara, but it talks about the two aspects in an indistinguishable manner. There does not seem to be any basic metaphysical distinction between them. When Brahman is beyond all attributes and remains just a metaphysical absolute then it is referred to as the Para Brahman, but when that very Brahman becomes epistemically active through its own power, namely Māyā, and epidemically creates and sustains the world and becomes immanent in it, then it is referred to as the Apara Brahman or Īśvara. Moreover, this Īśvara not only creates and sustains the world but it also controls it in a subtle manner. Now, it is impossible for the human mind to even imagine about the nature of Para Brahman as it has been indicated as that which is beyond the range of space, time, causality, language and reason. The moment one tries to imagine or talk about it, it comes within the realm of these parameters and hence it necessarily becomes a discourse about the Apara Brahman or Īśvara. In such a scenario, the moment one realizes the futility of one's efforts to transcend the limits of space, time, causality, language and

58 ...*bhrāmayan-sarva-bhūtāni yantrārūḍhāni māyayā,* Bhagavadgītā, 18-61.

reason, one naturally surrenders before the supreme controller of the world, namely Īśvara. This surrender before the unsurpassable jurisdiction and control of the Apara Brahman or Īśvara naturally leads to devotion to that Īśvara. When this devotion rises to the esoteric level, then by the grace of Īśvara one attains the intuitive knowledge of the nature of Brahman, and then only one becomes eligible to realize one's complete identity with Para Brahman i.e. liberation from the phenomenal cycle of birth and death. In this manner, Bhagavadgītā presents Brahman and Īśvara as the twin faces of a metaphysical absolute, which alone is the ultimate support and explanation of the phenomenal world and which alone is our highest goal and destiny.

2.2 Ātman and Jīvātman

The concept of Ātman primarily refers to the most basic and primary aspect of the self. However, self is commonly understood in the sense of the subject who is involved with the various decisions, actions and experiences associated with our mortal physical body. If so, then the self must be taken as undergoing various kinds of mental and physical experiences. In such a scenario, the various transcendental claims made by the Vedas regarding the nature of Ātman cannot be compatible with the empirical nature of the self. Hence, it is clear that the empirical self and subject cannot be treated as the true denotation of Ātman.

Now, the concept of Jīvātman refers to the empirical consciousness that identifies itself with the material body and believes itself to be the subject of all mental and physical actions and experiences. A Jīvātman, by definition, is that consciousness which is qualified by the internal organ or antaḥ-karaṇa. The internal organ consists of four faculties – manas, buddhi, citta and ahaṁkāra. Manas or mind stands for the passive receptive faculty of our consciousness that receives sensory information coming through the various sense organs. Buddhi or intellect refers to the active intelligence that analyses, correlates and takes various decisions. Citta stands for the recollective faculty where the mental impressions of all our thoughts and experiences are stored for future recollection and use. Ahaṁkāra or ego- principal is that faculty of our consciousness which appropriates all decisions, actions and experiences to itself, believing that all of them belong to it. The concept of a Jīvātman can never be devoid of its association with the internal organ and its four faculties. Therefore, a Jīvātman stands for the spiritually bound and ignorant state of the consciousness.

On the other hand, Ātman refers to the basic and pure aspect of our self and consciousness. A spiritually ignorant and bound person is unaware of this fundamental aspect of the self. It requires continuous and prolonged spiritual practice to become intuitively aware of the pure and fundamental aspect of the self, devoid of all association with the internal organ. It is with reference to this pure aspect of the self that the Vedic proclamations of its identity with the supreme Brahman are made. This Ātman is identical with Brahman. It is pure transcendent consciousness, completely beyond the range of space, time, causality, reason and language. This very consciousness, from the viewpoint of the individual is referred to as Ātman; but the same pure transcendent consciousness, from the viewpoint of the cosmos, has been called Brahman. The two are one and the same. They are identical, as proclaimed by the Upaniṣadic Mahāvākyas, namely *Tattvamasi, Aham brahmāsmi, Ayamātmā brahma* and

Prajñānaṁ brahma. That is to say, Brahman and Ātman are one and the same, but the same cannot be said for Ātman and Jīvātman. Ātman stands for the pure immutable transcendent consciousness, whereas Jīvātman refers to the empirical subject, who is the agent and experiencer of various mental and physical actions.

Let us now take a look at some of the illustrative stanzas from the Bhagavadgītā shedding light on the nature of Ātman and Jīvātman. Referring to the essential nature of the Ātman, Bhagavadgītā says that the Ātman residing within the various phenomenal beings is truly eternal in nature; there was never a time when it was not there and there will never be a time when it will not be there.[59] This Ātman is indestructible and undecaying. It is that with which everything is permeated. It is omnipresent. Not only that, it is also metaphysically immutable.[60] That is, it does go through any real metaphysical changes. Whatsoever change seems to be taking place in it, must be treated as basically epistemic in nature, because of its proclaimed immutable nature. This Ātman has also been declared *aprameya* by Bhagavadgītā.[61] It is said to be *aprameya* because it is beyond the reach of all the pramāṇas or the means of valid knowledge, such as perception, inference, etc. It is self-proven and the very ground of all possible proofs and discursive deliberations. It is the primary presupposition of all possible cognitive acts and experiences. It is self-revealing. Just as a light source does not require another light source to make it seen, similarly the Ātman does not require any other

---

59 *...sarve vayamataḥ param,* Bhagavadgītā, 2-12.

60 *...vināśam-avyayasya-asya na kaścit-kartumarhati,* Bhagavadgītā, 2-17.

61 *...anāśino-aprameyasya...,* Bhagavadgītā, 2-18.

consciousness to show its existence. It is that consciousness itself which makes possible all cognitive acts and experiences.

Further, Bhagavadgītā emphatically points out the aloofness of Ātman from all activities undertaken by the physical body.[62] It is an illusion to think that it is the agent responsible for various actions done by the body. The truth is that the Ātman remains completely untouched by the activities of the body and the mind, just as the light which shows good and bad things and activities, itself remains untouched by goodness and badness of those things and activities. This Ātman is eternal, all permeating, immovable and ever unchanged.[63] Since the Ātman transcends time, therefore it has no beginning or end in time. As such, the Ātman is said to be eternal. In its true nature, the Ātman is not limited by the physical body. The physical body is only its temporary qualification and in reality, it is omnipresent and all permeating. Being omnipresent, it logically turns out to be immovable. Its omnipresence and immovability rule out the possibility of changes taking place in it in a true metaphysical sense.

This Ātman is the Unmanifest. It is beyond the range of all cognitive comprehension and it is also beyond all changes and corruptions.[64] It is said to be the *avyakta* or Unmanifest, since its true nature is never manifested and revealed in the phenomenal world and also because the whole cosmos lies implicitly latent within it before the epistemic creation of the world by God. It is said to be beyond all cognitive comprehension, because it is a metaphysical absolute in its

---

62 *...ubhau tau na vijānīto nāyaṁ hanti na hanyate,* Bhagavadgītā, 2-19.

63 *...nityaḥ sarva-gataḥ sthāṇur-acaloyaṁ sanātanaḥ,* Bhagavadgītā, 2-24.

64 *...avyaktoyam-acintyoyam-avikāryoyam-ucyate,* Bhagavadgītā, 2-25.

pure nature. Being so, there is no possibility of the duality of subject and object, which is the inalienable characteristic of cognitive comprehension. As such, there cannot be any cognitive comprehension of the pure nature of the Ātman. Further, being a metaphysical absolute, the Ātman is beyond the realm of space, time, causality and change, which means it is immutable and there can be no change or corruption in it. It is also pointed out beautifully in the Bhagavadgītā that a person who has gained the intuitive realization of the pure and transcendent nature of Brahman, has no use of the Vedas, even though the Vedas are considered the ultimate source of esoteric knowledge related to all phenomenal and spiritual goals and objectives.[65] It is said to be so because the Ātman, being identical with Brahman, is itself unconditioned infinite existence, consciousness and bliss, as well as the metaphysical support and epistemic source of all phenomenal entities. As such, for the Brahman realized person there can be nothing that lies outside his Self or Ātman. Hence, even the Vedas have nothing to offer him.

Since the Ātman or Brahman is the metaphysical source and support of the entire cosmos, therefore it is immanent in all the entities of the world. Being so, the Brahman realized person witnesses the omnipresence of Brahman through all the entities of the world and hence remains even-minded towards all of them, irrespective of their varying qualities and characteristics.[66]

In the light of above discussion, it is clear that Ātman refers to the most fundamental metaphysical aspect of our self, that is actually identical with the transcendent absolute,

---

[65] Bhagavadgītā, 2-46.

[66] ...*paṇḍitāḥ sama-darśinaḥ,* Bhagavadgītā, 5-18.

namely Brahman. The same ontological reality is known as Ātman from the individual perspective and Brahman from the cosmic perspective. On the other hand, Jīvātman or the empirical self refers to the illusion of the pure consciousness being qualified by the internal organ in terms of its four faculties. The illusory appearance of the Jīvātman is the result of spiritual ignorance, springing from the epistemic activity of Māyā. This illusory epistemic activity itself takes place through the will and power of Brahman alone. It cannot be otherwise, since Brahman or Ātman alone is the metaphysical absolute and the world cannot have any explanation and metaphysical ground other than that Brahman itself. Therefore, for the Brahman realized person, there can be no limited individual identity related with the material body. Such a person witnesses Brahman alone in all phenomenal entities and also finds all entities being metaphysically grounded in that supreme Brahman alone.

2.3 Prakṛiti and its Guṇas

The concepts of Prakṛti and Puruṣa have repeatedly been discussed in the Bhagavadgītā. This certainly shows that they have a very important place in its metaphysical framework. The term Sāṅkhya too has been used repeatedly in the Bhagavadgītā. Due to the repeated use of these terms, very often people come to believe that Bhagavad-Gītā has used the metaphysical framework of Sāṅkhya philosophy.

However, it needs to be clarified at the outset that such an impression is quite misleading. One must clearly understand the connotations of these terms in the context of Bhagavadgītā and in the context of Sāṅkhya. Let us first take the case of Sāṅkhya philosophy. Sāṅkhya philosophy was propounded by sage Kapila and the earliest text of Sāṅkhya is believed to be Sāṅkhya-sūtra.[67] However, this text is no longer available. The earliest text of Sāṅkhya which is available is Sāṅkhya-kārikā by Īśvarakṛṣṇa. The term Sāṅkhya is closely related with the term saṅkhyā or number. In this philosophy the enumeration of the basic metaphysical categories is highlighted. There are two ultimate categories, namely Puruṣa and Prakṛti, where the former stands for transcendent principle of pure consciousness and the latter stands for the ultimate material principle. Taking the evolutes of Prakṛti also into consideration, the total number of categories comes to twenty-five. Considering only the material categories, their total number is twenty-four, including Prakṛti. Thus, there are twenty-three material evolutes of Prakṛti. Puruṣa is the only spiritual principle of consciousness.

Puruṣa, in the Sāṅkhya philosophy, is the transcendent principle of consciousness. That is, it is supposed to be beyond space, time, causality, etc. It is also believed to be immutable i.e. beyond all changes. It is only pure consciousness, having no element of bliss within it. It is also believed to be omnipresent. However, it is also believed to be infinite in number. This Puruṣa is the only source of consciousness in this philosophy. Further, being immutable, it never interacts with any other entity in the metaphysical sense. Specifically, it has no direct interaction with Prakṛti and its evolutes.

In fact, despite its ontological immutability, it can suffer from epistemic illusion, due to which it apparently starts identifying itself with the material principles. This misidentification leads to its spiritual and karmic bondage,

---

[67] Sharma, C. D., *A Critical Survey of Indian Philosophy,* MLBD, Delhi, 1991, p. 149.

which is basically rooted in its spiritual ignorance about its own nature and its own absolute distinction from Prakṛti and all its material evolutes. So, the bondage of Puruṣa in Sāṅkhya philosophy is a matter of spiritual ignorance and its resultant illusion about the nature of the self. As such, the liberation of Puruṣa in Sāṅkhya philosophy must also be only epistemic in nature. Regarding Puruṣa, C. D. Sharma says - *"Really speaking, it is above time and space, merit and demerit, bondage and liberation. It is only when it mistakes its reflection in the buddhi for itself and identifies itself wrongly with the internal organ -the intellect, the ego and the mind, that it is said to be bound. It is the ego, and not the Puruṣa, which is bound. When the Puruṣa realizes its own pure nature, it gets liberated which in fact it always was. Hence, bondage is due to ignorance or non-discrimination between the self and the not-self and liberation is due to right knowledge or discrimination between the self and the not-self."*[68]

Thus, the Puruṣa of Sāṅkhya is an immutable and transcendent ontological category of pure consciousness. It is by itself an ultimate and completely independent metaphysical category. There is nothing over and above it. Moreover, there are infinite number of such transcendent Puruṣas.

The Prakṛti of Sāṅkhya is an ultimate material principle, which serves as the ultimate cause and explanation of all material evolutes and entities. All twenty-three material categories evolve out of Prakṛti itself and this sequential evolution of all the categories is called the creation of the material world. This Prakṛti is constituted by three kinds of material energies, which are called its *guṇas*. The three guṇas

[68] Sharma, C. D., *A Critical Survey of Indian Philosophy*, MLBD, Delhi, 1991, p. 163.

are sattva, rajas and tamas. Technically, Prakṛti refers to that specific state of the guṇas when they are in a state of mutual equilibrium. In this state, the guṇas do not transform into other types of guṇas. That is, sattva changes into sattva only and similarly for the other two guṇas. This kind of transformation of the guṇas is known as homogeneous transformation or *sarūpa pariṇāma.* So, Prakṛti stands for the homogeneous transformative state of the guṇas. It is beginningless and the source of all material principles. Hence, it is one only.

According to Sāṅkhya, this state of the equilibrium of the guṇas gets disturbed by the *saṁyogābhāsa* of Puruṣa and Prakṛti i.e. the semblance of contact between Puruṣa and Prakṛti.[69] This is not a real contact between them, but only an appearance of contact between them. Sāṅkhya offers the analogy of cooperation between a lame and a blind person to reach a common destination. Now, once the equilibrium of the guṇas gets disturbed, *virūpa pariṇāma* or heterogeneous transformation of the guṇas starts taking place, due to which one kind of guṇa gets transformed into another type of guṇa. This kind of transformation starts the process of evolution of Prakṛti, as a result of which various material ontological categories, starting with Mahat, come into effect. Now, all material entities are ultimately constituted by various kinds of combinations of the three guṇas, where any one of them may be dominating over the other two. Further, the three guṇas have their own peculiar characteristics, which are exhibited by the various material entities in varying degrees.

The above discussion presented a brief outline of the metaphysical framework of the Sāṅkhya philosophy,

---

[69] Sharma, C. D., *A Critical Survey of Indian Philosophy,* MLBD, Delhi, 1991, p. 159.

especially with respect to the concepts of Puruṣa and Prakṛti. Now, let us try to see the nature of these concepts, as presented in the Bhagavad-Gītā. As far as the term Sāṅkhya is concerned, it has been used primarily in the sense of right knowledge, especially in the sense of spiritual metaphysics. That is, in the Bhagavadgītā, Sāṅkhya has been used to refer to the right understanding of the spiritual metaphysics of the cosmos. The metaphysical framework of Bhagavadgītā is an absolutist framework, where the supreme metaphysical category has been called Brahman and Ātman. In contrast, the metaphysical framework of the Sāṅkhya philosophy is dualistic where there are two distinct ultimate metaphysical categories, namely Puruṣa and Prakṛti. Not only are there two kinds of ultimate realities, but numerically speaking, there are infinite number of ultimate realities in Sāṅkhya, because there are infinite number of Puruṣas.

Now, let us take a look at the concept of Puruṣa, as given in Bhagavadgītā. Here, we find three distinct connotations of the term Puruṣa. First of all, it refers to the empirical self, which is the subject of various mental and physical actions and experiences. Naturally, this sense of Puruṣa goes through various kinds of changes and it represents the most superficial aspect of the self. So, the concept of Puruṣa associated with the empirical self is subject to changes of all sorts and it is that sense of self with which everyone is naturally acquainted. The next sense of Puruṣa refers to the witness aspect of the self. It is that aspect of the self which is consciousness in its pure aspect, dissociated from the mental and physical aspects of our personality. The pure aspect of our consciousness, as delimited by our phenomenal individuality, is this second aspect of the Puruṣa. This aspect of the self is basically one with the highest reality or Brahman, except for its contingent qualification by the phenomenal individuality. Just as the space delimited by a jar may be comprehended as separate from the universal space just because of its contingent qualification by the jar, even though it is actually one and inseparable from the universal space, similarly the witness aspect of the self remains untouched by the contingent phenomenal individuality. Ontologically speaking, it is but one with the supreme Brahman or Ātman.

The third and the highest aspect of the self is that transcendent, universal, pure consciousness which lies beyond the realms of space, time, causality, duality, reason and language. It has no contingent qualifications attached to it. It is the supreme ontological absolute. It is what is referred to as Brahman and Ātman. Therefore, it has been called *Puruṣottama,* or the supreme Puruṣa, in Bhagavad-Gītā. Hence, it can be clearly seen that the Sāṅkhya concept of Puruṣa is very different from that which has been presented in Bhagavad-Gītā. There is a hierarchy of the notion of Puruṣa in Bhagavad-Gītā, which is pluralistic at the bottom, but universalistic and absolutist at the top, whereas in Sāṅkhya philosophy there are just infinite number of similar transcendent Puruṣas. The Sāṅkhya account of Puruṣa makes explaining the empirical aspect of self logically difficult. It also leads to the objection of qualitative monism and quantitative pluralism. Therefore, one should not think about the concept of Puruṣa being the same in the Bhagavadgītā and the Sāṅkhya philosophy. The highest aspect of Puruṣa in Bhagavadgītā is identical with the supreme and transcendent ontologically absolute category of Brahman and Ātman, which are one and the same.

Now, the concept of Prakṛti and its guṇas, as presented in the Bhagavadgītā, is compatible with its absolutist metaphysical framework. That is, it does not present a challenge to the supremeness of Brahman. It is subsumed within the ontological fold of Brahman. Here Prakṛti is presented as the inalienable and inscrutable power of Brahman, through which the epistemic creation of the whole cosmos, consisting of material and spiritual entities, is effected. Two kinds of Prakṛti are indicated in Bhagavadgītā - the higher or *Parā* and the lower or *Aparā.* The higher Prakṛti is instrumental in the epistemic creation of the individual souls, whereas the lower Prakṛti is instrumental in the epistemic creation of the non-conscious and material entities of the world. These twin aspects of Prakṛti, taken together, represent Māyā, the inalienable and inscrutable power of Brahman. This account of Prakṛti is clearly incomparable with the Sāṅkhya account of Prakṛti, where it is depicted as an independent ultimate material category, which has nothing to do with consciousness. The Sāṅkhya account evolution of Prakṛti, springing from the semblance of contact between Puruṣa and Prakṛti, is highly problematic and logically indefensible. In contrast, the Bhagavadgītā account of Prakṛti faces no such problem because there it is the inalienable power of Brahman and as such, it is completely under the control of the infinite intelligence of Brahman.

As for the guṇas, the lower Prakṛti of Bhagavadgītā consists of the three guṇas and therefore, the characteristics of the three guṇas get reflected in the various material entities of the world. To this extent, there is similarity with the Sāṅkhya account of the guṇas but the higher Prakṛti of Bhagavadgītā explains the individual souls as well. This aspect of Prakṛti is completely unimaginable in the case of Sāṅkhya philosophy.

Thus, there is no possibility of treating the Prakṛti of Sāṅkhya and the Prakṛti of Bhagavadgītā to be at par with each other.

In the light of above discussion, it can be clearly seen that the metaphysical framework of Bhagavadgītā is unique in many ways and it certainly cannot be identified with the metaphysical framework of Sāṅkhya philosophy. The concepts of Prakṛti and Puruṣa are vastly different in them. Now, let us try to take a look at some of the illustrative stanzas of Bhagavadgītā which throw some light on the concept of Prakṛti and its guṇas.

Bhagavadgītā refers to Vedas as having a content which deals with the three guṇas and hence Arjuna is exhorted to transcend the realm of the three guṇas.[70] The guṇas are responsible for the characteristics and activities pertaining to all material entities and the Vedas primarily deal with the attainment of various goals related to the phenomenal world and subtle worlds. It is not possible to attain the highest spiritual realization as long as one remains entangled with matters related with the three guṇas. Therefore, Arjuna is exhorted to transcend the guṇas and the Vedas in order to attain the highest spiritual goal. Further, Bhagavadgītā emphasizes the point that all the phenomenal activities, both external and internal, take place on account of the guṇas alone, but because of the ego principle one comes to believe that the agency of those actions actually belongs to him.[71] Those having spiritual insight into the nature of the guṇas do not get mesmerized by the characteristics and activities effected by them at the phenomenal plane.[72] They are aware of the fact that

---

[70] *traiguṇya-viṣayā vedā nistraiguṇyo bhavārjuna...*, Bhagavadgītā, 2-45.

[71] *prakṛteḥ kriyamāṇāni guṇaiḥ karmāṇi sarvaśaḥ...*, Bhagavadgītā, 3-27.

[72] *guṇā guṇeṣu vartanta iti matvā na sajjate ...*, Bhagavadgītā, 3-28.

their true self is not involved with the material characteristics and activities. As a result of this knowledge and conviction, they so not get attached to the material qualities and activities. On the other hand, those who lack such spiritual insight, are easily be fooled by the phenomenal exhibition of material qualities and activities and a result of that, they easily get attached to the various material qualities and activities.[73] The spiritually ignorant persons take themselves to be the real agents of material activities and the real experiencer of material qualities. Thinking so, they easily get attached to the worldly activities and experiences. The transcendent nature of both Prakṛti and Puruṣa are clearly indicated in Bhagavadgītā. Both are said to be beginningless.[74] They are said to be beginningless in the sense that Prakṛti, being the inalienable power of Brahman, transcends time; and Puruṣa, being the epistemic individualization of Brahman, through the power of Parā Prakṛti or Māyā, too becomes ontologically identical with Brahman and therefore, Puruṣa also transcends time. That is, both Puruṣa and Prakṛti, are ontologically rooted in Brahman and hence, in their basic nature, both transcend time. Further, all the phenomenal pluralities, both mental and physical, as well as their characteristic features, become possible due the instrumentality of Prakṛti. Right from the four faculties of the internal organ up to the grossest material things, everything is ultimately a proximate or distant effect of Prakṛti only.

Prakṛti is responsible for the epistemic manifestation of all the individual souls as well as all material entities. Even space and time have their apparent existence due to Prakṛti. The

---

[73] *prakṛter-guṇa-sammūḍhāḥ sajjante guṇakarmasu ..,* Bhagavadgītā, 3-29.

[74] *prakṛtiṁ puruṣaṁ caiva viddhy-anādī ubhāvapi,*
vikārāṁś-ca guṇāś-caiva viddhi prakṛti-sambhavān, Bhagavadgītā, 13-19.

appearance of causality is but a function of space and time. Therefore, the appearances of cause, effect and the agency of actions, all owe their possibility to the ultimate causality of Prakṛti alone.[75] In fact, all the parameters of the phenomenal world, namely space, time, causality, ego sense, all mental and material attributes etc. become possible only through the causality of Prakṛti, the inscrutable and inalienable power of Brahman. This Prakṛti may also be understood as Māyā. In one of its aspects, Puruṣa refers to the individual soul which falls into the spiritual illusion of identifying itself with the empirical self and therefore that Puruṣa is virtually grounded in and sustained by Prakṛti. Being thus grounded in Prakṛti, the Puruṣa experiences the guṇas of Prakṛti, as manifesting through the various mental and material states and entities. As a result of its association with the various guṇas, the Puruṣa, as empirical self, goes through the cycle of various good and bad births.[76] The right understanding of the nature of Puruṣa, Prakṛti and the guṇas leads one to freedom from the cycle of birth and death. Even though that person may be performing all his phenomenal duties in the world, he gets released from the cycle of transmigration.[77]

The person who understands and sees Prakṛti alone as the real agent behind all phenomenal activities does not fall into spiritual ignorance and illusion. He remains convinced of the fact of his soul's aloofness from all activities i.e. he fully knows that his soul or self is not the real agent of any action, despite the opposite illusory appearance.[78] This Prakṛti is the source of

---

[75] *kārya-karaṇa-kartṛtve hetuḥ prakṛtir-ucyate ...,* Bhagavadgītā, 13-20.

[76] *puruṣaḥ prakṛtistho hi bhuṅkte prakṛtijān- guṇān,*

kāraṇaṁ guṇa-saṅgo'sya sadasad-yoni-janmasu, Bhagavadgītā, 13-21.

[77] Ibid., 13-23.

[78] *prakṛtyaiva ca karmāṇi kriyamāṇāni sarvaśaḥ,*

the three guṇas, namely sattva, rajas and tamas. These three guṇas are responsible for binding the immutable consciousness, the soul, to the material body through epistemic illusion.[79] Out of these three guṇas, sattva is the purest one and it has the capacity to give spiritual enlightenment, but it is also binding through the sense of attachment to bliss and sense of ego related with one's knowledge.[80] The rajas guṇa leads to attachments of various kinds and it is itself the result of desires for phenomenal things and experiences. It binds the soul karmically to all phenomenal actions and their results.[81] That is, desires for phenomenal experiences are the root cause of the soul's karmic bondage. Of course, all such desires themselves spring from the still more basic spiritual ignorance about the real nature of the self and the resultant misidentification of the self with the material body. Tamas guṇa is rooted in ignorance and leads to the delusion of the individual soul. It binds the soul through delusion, laziness and sleep.[82]

Sattva guṇa propels one to engage in activities that provide blissful experiences; rajas guṇa stimulates one to engage in such activities which enhance one's sense of ego, while tamas guṇa covers up one's knowledge and leads to all sorts of delusions and laziness.[83] These three guṇas constantly keep on changing their mutual strengths, as a result of which sometimes sattva dominates over the other two, sometimes

---

yaḥ paśyati tathātmānam-akartāraṁ sa paśyati, Bhagavadgītā, 13-29.

79 *sattvaṁ rajas-tama iti guṇāḥ prakṛti-sambhavāḥ ...,* Bhagavadgītā, 14-5.

80 *tatra sattvaṁ nirmalatvāt-prakāśkam-anāmayam ..,* Bhagavadgītā, 14-6.

81 *rajo rāgātmakaṁ viddhi tṛṣṇā-saṅga-samudbhavam...,* Bhagavadgītā, 14-7.

82 *tamastv-ajñānajaṁ viddhi mohanaṁ sarva-dehinām..,* Bhagavadgītā, 14-8.

83 Ibid., 14-9.

rajas dominates over the other two and sometimes tamas dominates over the other two.[84]

Whenever there is an affluence of consciousness and discrimination in the internal organ, senses and the body, one should understand that sattva guṇa is dominating over the other guṇas.[85] That is, the preponderance of knowledge and discrimination at given point of time is an indicator of the dominance of sattva guṇa. When there is the dominance of rajas guṇa, one experiences a pronounced increase in one's selfishness, greed, desire for sensory pleasures and there is total loss of peace of mind.[86] That is, the dominance of rajas propels one to vigorously engage in selfishly motivated actions for the sake of achieving various kinds of sense pleasures and enhancing one's sense of ego. When there is a preponderance of tamas, one is engulfed by a sense of confusion and ignorance in one's mind, senses and internal organ. One turns away from the performance of one's duties and there is lack of sufficient zeal. One suffers from overpowering sleep and laziness.[87]

The state of dominance of the guṇas at the time of death is critical in deciding the nature of one's future life form as well as the sphere of one's existence. If sattva is preponderant at the point of death, the next birth takes place in higher realms of existence, like heaven or other higher spiritual realms. If rajas dominate at the time of death, the next birth is likely to be at the phenomenal plane of human beings, who are always engaged in activities aimed at pleasant experiences. But, if

[84] Ibid., 14-10.

[85] Ibid., 14-11.

[86] Ibid., 14-12.

[87] Ibid., 14-13.

tamas dominates at the time of death, the future birth may be in the form of animals and other lower life forms.[88] Actions dominated by the sattva guṇa lead to karmic results which give knowledge, discrimination, peace and bliss; actions dominated by rajas lead to suffering and misery, whereas actions dominated by tamas lead to ignorance and confusion.[89]

When a person has a firm conviction about the fact that the real agency of all actions belongs only to the three guṇas and the pure consciousness of the soul is not involved in any actions, then that person attains identity with Brahman and thus attains liberation. When that person has the right knowledge about that spiritual category which transcends all the three guṇas, he attains to the highest liberation i.e. realization of one's identity with Brahman.[90] The characteristic feature of sattva is clarity of mind, consciousness, knowledge and discrimination. The sign of rajas is the impetus to engage in various kinds of activities, whereas the mark of tamas is delusion, confusion, sloth and ignorance. When a person does not hate and dislike the characteristic features of any of the guṇas and also does not desire for the removal of those characteristic features, then that person transcends the guṇas and he earns the designation of a *guṇātīta*.[91] A person who has transcended all the three guṇas is always aware of the fact that the soul is beyond all the guṇas and is never engaged with any

---

88 Ibid., 14-14,15.

89 Ibid., 14-16.

90 *nānyaṁ guṇebhyaḥ kartāraṁ yadā draṣṭānupaśyati,*
guṇebhyaś-ca paraṁ vetti madbhāvaṁ sodhigacchati, Bhagavadgītā, 14-19.

91 *prakāśaṁ ca pravṛttiṁ ca mohameva ca pāṇḍava,*
na dveṣṭi sampravṛittāni na nivṛttāni kāṅkṣati, Bhagavadgītā, 14-22.
and
...sarvārambha-parityāgī guṇātītaḥ sa ucyate, Bhagavadgītā, 14-25.

activity. Such a person remains even minded in the face of sensory pleasures and pains. For him, there is no difference between mud and gold. He remains indifferent to both honour and insult. He is even minded towards all things, situations and experiences, because he is intuitively aware of the transcendent nature of the Ātman and Brahman, as well as the phenomenal show and play of Prakṛti and its guṇas. Such a person is firmly established in his identity with Brahman.[92]

One's faith or *śraddhā* can be of three types, depending on the preponderance of a guṇa in the internal organ. If sattva dominates in the internal organ, then that person worships divine deities. If rajas dominate in the internal organ, then the person worships *yakṣas* and demons. If tamas dominates, then that person worships ghosts and similar other beings.[93] Similarly, the kind of foods liked by a person is also influenced by the dominate guṇa in that person. If sattva is dominant in a person, then he would like foods which are naturally tasty, beneficial for health, juicy, mild in taste and enduring.[94] A person who is dominated by rajas would like foods that are salty, pungent, sour, bitter, hot and responsible for various kinds of diseases and suffering.[95] In case of a person dominated by tamas, he would like foods that are half cooked, foul smelling, fermented and impure.[96] Similarly, *yajña* or a religious sacrifice also can be of three types, as influenced by the predominant guṇa. If a person's nature is dominated by the sattva guṇa, he would like to perform religious rituals that are prescribed by the scriptures and he would do it as a matter

[92] Ibid., 14-23,24,25.

[93] Ibid., 17-4.

[94] Ibid., 17-8.

[95] Ibid., 17-9.

[96] Ibid., 17-10.

of duty, without the desire for any kind of results.[97] Such religious sacrifices are said to be *sāttvika.* But, when a religious sacrifice is performed for the sake of showing off one's religiosity to others or even for the fulfilment of various worldly desires, that sacrifice is considered *rājasika* in nature.[98] A religious sacrifice in which the scriptural prescriptions are not followed, which is devoid of sacred chants and charity, and also lacking in true faith, should be considered *tāmasika* in nature.[99]

Tapas or austerity too is of three kinds, depending on the preponderance of a particular guṇa in a person. Moreover, austerity is of three levels, namely that of body, speech and mind. Devotion towards deities, spiritual persons, one's guru, purity, simplicity, celibacy and non-violence, are considered the sāttvika austerity of the body.[100] Sāttvika austerity of speech consists of speaking the truth, speaking that which is beneficial, the study of scriptures and reciting and repeating the names of God.[101] The sāttvika austerity of the mind consists of blissfulness and tranquility of the mind, constant remembrance of God, having control over the internal organ and the purity of one's thoughts.[102] The austerity that is done for the sake of gaining honour and respect, or done out of sheer hypocrisy, or due to any other selfish reason, is considered rājasika austerity.[103] The austerity that is done out of foolish adamance, that is painful and mortifying to the body and

---

97 Ibid., 17-11.

98 Ibid., 17-12.

99 Ibid., 17-13.

100 Ibid., 17-14.

101 Ibid., 17-15.

102 Ibid., 17-16.

103 Ibid., 17-18.

mind, or that is done for the sake of bringing harm to others, is considered tāmasika austerity.[104]

Similarly, depending on the preponderance of each guṇa, *dāna* or charity too is said to be of three kinds - sāttvika, rājasika and tāmasika. When charity is done with the conviction that it is a duty to be carried out and while giving charity one takes due consideration of the circumstances and worthiness of the receiver, such that it is given to a person who is not in a position to return the favour, that charity is considered sāttvika in nature.[105] When charity is done in a half-hearted manner, or it is aimed at getting some return favour, or it is done for the sake of some objectives to be realized, then it becomes a case of rājasika charity.[106] The charity which is given without giving due consideration to the circumstances, and is devoid of respect and humility, or is imparted to unsuitable recipients, is considered tāmasika in nature.[107]

Now, *tyāga* or leaving behind something is also of three kinds, depending on the dominance of some particular guṇa. But it should not be confused with formal renunciation. When a person gives up one's duties due to ignorance and confusion then this kind of giving up is said to be tāmasika in nature.[108] But, when a person starts thinking of all actions as sources of suffering and as a result of such notion, gives up one's duties to avoid pain and suffering to the body, then it becomes a rājasika case of giving up actions.[109] However, when a person

---

[104] Ibid., 17-19.

[105] Ibid., 17-20.

[106] Ibid., 17-21.

[107] Ibid., 17-22.

[108] Ibid., 18-7.

[109] Ibid., 18-8.

understands the sanctity of the duties prescribed by scriptures and tradition and hence carries out his duties, only out of a sense of duty, without having any attachment to the results of those actions, then the giving up of all attachment to results of actions is called sāttvika in nature.[110] Now, corresponding to the preponderance of each particular guṇa, knowledge too can be classified into three types. The knowledge through which one sees God as manifesting through all entities in an indivisible manner, is said to be sāttvika knowledge.[111] The knowledge through which we see plurality in the world and feel all entities to have different characteristics, is said to be rājasika knowledge.[112] When a person is totally obsessed with his physical personality and body, believing that alone to be the ultimate reality, his knowledge is considered tāmasika.[113] That karma or action which is done because it has been prescribed by the scriptures as one's duty and is performed without any attachment to its result, and is completely free from attachment and aversion, comes under the category of sāttvika action.[114] The action which is laborious and done for the sake of enjoying sense pleasures, and is done in an egotistic manner, is considered as rājasika action.[115] That action which is performed out of ignorance, without any consideration for its result, likely adverse effects, resulting violence and one's own capability, is believed to be tāmasika in nature.[116] Similarly, *kartā* or the agent of action also is of three types,

---

[110] Ibid., 18-9.

[111] Ibid., 18-20.

[112] Ibid., 18-21.

[113] Ibid., 18-22.

[114] Ibid., 18-23.

[115] Ibid., 18-24.

[116] Ibid., 18-25.

corresponding to the dominance of each guṇa. A person who engages in actions with zeal and patience, who is free from attachment to the result of actions, who never speaks in an egotistic manner and remains equipoised in the face of success and failure, is said to be a sāttvika agent.[117] When a person performs actions out of greed and attachment, for hurting other people and is oscillating between pleasure and pain, he comes under the category of rājasika agent.[118] A person who is uncultured, full of ego, cunning, harmful to other person's livelihood, miserable and lazy, is considered a tāmasika agent of actions.[119]

Similarly, according to the dominance of each guṇa, there are correspondingly three kinds of intelligence and wisdom. The intelligence which properly understands the nature of the paths of worldly upliftment and spiritual upliftment, the distinction between duties and non-duties, fear and fearlessness and also the distinction between spiritual bondage and liberation, is considered sāttvika intelligence and wisdom.[120] The intelligence that does not properly comprehend the distinction between righteousness and non-righteousness and also between duties and non-duties, is said to be rājasika intelligence and wisdom.[121] The intelligence which understands duties as non-duties and vice-versa and similarly has contrary understanding of various kinds of

[117] Ibid., 18-26.

[118] Ibid., 18-27.

[119] Ibid., 18-28.

[120] Ibid., 18-30.

[121] Ibid., 18-31.

actions, comes under the category of tāmasika intelligence and wisdom.[122]

In the light of above discussion, one can clearly understand the metaphysical framework of the Bhagavadgītā. To sum up the discussion, we can point out the metaphysically absolutist framework inherent in Bhagavadgītā. Despite its absolutist metaphysics, it explains the manifestation of the individual souls and the material entities. It also highlights the supreme status of God and makes room for devotion and grace. Moreover, it explains the mental and physical variety of the phenomenal world with the help of the three guṇas of Prakṛti. In this way the metaphysical framework of Bhagavadgītā is certainly remarkable and adds much to the clarification of the Vedic tradition.

---

[122] Ibid., 18-32.

Chapter 3:
Cosmic Framework of Tao-Teh Ching

Amongst the various ancient spiritual traditions of China, Taoism or Daoism represents perhaps the most important religious philosophical tradition. It is evident from the tradition's name itself that the belief and practices of Taoism are rooted in the concept of Tao. It is believed to be propounded by Lao-Tze. He is also known as Lao-Tse, Lao-Tzu and Laodi. In Chinese language, 'Lao-Tze' means old master. His original name was Li, which literally means the fruit plum. He was called Li because of his birth under a plum tree. His period mostly spans over the sixth century BCE, although he is usually believed to be born in 604 BCE.

The term 'Tao' had not been used by Lao-Tze for the first time. It had been in use in the Chinese tradition even before Lao-Tze in various contexts. Before the period of Lao-Tze this term was used in different senses by different religious, philosophical, social and political schools in China. Even though it had different connotations in the context of different schools, there was something common to all the uses of the term. That common point was the fact that in all its varied uses, it always referred to the central principle of the given school. That is, the term 'Tao' always referred to the most important metaphysical or social or moral or political or philosophical principle. However, none of the earlier schools using the term 'Tao' had a name centred around this concept. It was only in the case of the thought propounded by Lao-Tze that it came to be named over the concept of Tao.

Taoism has two distinct branches, namely Tao-Chia and Tao-Chiao. The two streams of Taoism are both conceptually and chronologically distinct. Tao-Chia stands for the historically earlier branch of Taoism. It is associated with the works and ideas of Lao-Tze and his chief disciple, Chuang-Tzu. It deals mostly with metaphysical, spiritual and moral ideas. It deals with deep philosophical issues. Therefore, Tao-Chia is also known as philosophical Taoism. On the other hand, Tao-Chiao comes much later historically. Its chief propounder was Chang-Ling, belonging to the second century CE, the period of the Han dynasty in China. Its focus was very different compared to the earlier Taoism. It dealt mostly with mystical and magical ideas, aiming at the longevity and even divinization and immortality of the physical body. In this effort, it dealt with various kinds of breath exercises, the use of esoteric medicinal plants and chemicals, as well as mystical religious ritual practices.

The basic scripture of Taoism is Tao-Teh-Ching. Just as Tao is also written as Dao, similarly Teh is also written as Te, and Ching is also written as King. Thus, Tao-Teh-Ching may also be written as Tao-Te-King. The term Ching or King basically means text, classic or scripture. This text comprises of almost five thousand pictographic characters, where each character conveys a complex idea, which is usually open to different interpretations. The text consists of eighty-one chapters and each chapter consists of many pictographic characters. The text is also divided into two sections - Tao-Ching and Teh-Ching, which may be roughly understood as the classic of the Tao and the classic of the Teh. Tao-Ching consists of the first thirty-seven chapters, whereas Teh-Ching consists of all the remaining chapters of the Tao-Teh-Ching.

There is a mythological anecdote about the origin of this text. The Chinese tradition believes that once Lao-Tze was going towards the west of China and he has to cross the valley of a mountain. When he was about to cross the valley, the presiding deity of that valley appeared before him and stopped him from proceeding further. When Lao-Tze questioned him about the reason for doing that, he was told that he could be allowed to proceed ahead only if he answered correctly some questions. Lao-Tze agreed to this condition and a long dialogue took place between the two. Ultimately, the deity was fully satisfied by his answers and gave him permission to go ahead. However, before Lao-Tze could actually leave that place, the deity persuaded him to put down in writing the various matters discussed by them for the benefit of the future generations. Lao-Tze humbly agreed to this request and that is how the short text Tao-Teh-Ching was authored.

The other important text of the Tao-Chia school of Taoism is known as the Chuang-Tzu book, which was authored by Chuang-Tzu, one of the chief disciples of Lao-Tze. This text is very important because it seeks to resolve many of the unstated riddles thrown up by the Tao-Teh-Ching. Specifically, it contributes significantly to the metaphysical framework indicated by the Tao-Teh-Ching.

3.1 The Concept of Tao

The term 'Tao' has varied connotations, but the primary connotation is 'the way.' The secondary connotations of the term are Heaven, the Almighty ruler, the Self-so (tzu-jan) and the One. Conjoining the primary and secondary connotations of Tao gives us various shades of meaning of the Tao, such as the way of nature or the way of being or the way things are or the way of process and reality or the way of the heaven. The primary connotation of Tao as the way has some very important logical implications. Whatever may be the secondary connotations of the term, the primary meaning of the term shows that there are two reference points for the use of this term. The first reference point is starting point of some sort of a journey, that has to be traversed through that way. The second reference point is the ultimate destination up to which the way has to take us and the journey has to be completed. Thus, the term Tao primarily shows that there is a journey to be completed and there is a way through which that journey has to be completed. Any way is never a way to nowhere. It is always a way from somewhere and to somewhere. On the other hand, the primary connotation of Teh is virtue. Now, the exact nature and description of that origin point and destination point is a matter of debatable interpretations. The best method of going about it is to take the help of the primary text itself for understanding the nature of the origin point, the destination points and the way leading to that destination point.

The very first statement of Tao-Teh-Ching tries to show the bewildering point that if one can go through or reach a certain ontological entity, then that entity cannot be unchanging in nature.[123] The moot point is that if some entity can be interacted with any other entity in any manner, then there is bound to be some degree of change in it, which means if something is unchangeable then there can be no possibility of anyone or anything reaching it or interacting with it. Hence,

---

123 Legge, James, Tr. *Tao-Teh-Ching*, 1-1, www.FreeSpiritualEbooks.com, 2008.

the real Tao must be that which cannot be reached and there cannot be any interaction with it. Similarly, it must also be beyond the possibility of naming i.e. beyond the realm of language.[124] The necessity of Tao being beyond the realm of naming and language can be understood in light of the obvious fact that language operates in the realm of space, time and plurality, whereas Tao is the unchanging reality and therefore it must be transcendent to all these categories. Being so, it is clear that it must be beyond the realm of language.

There are two aspects of the Tao. The aspect which is beyond naming, that is, the aspect which is beyond all the phenomenal categories, such as space, time, causality, reason and language, is that supreme ontological ground from which everything arises.[125] This means that it must be an ontological absolute. Its ontological absoluteness means there is no existence of anything other than that. On the other hand, that aspect of the Tao which can be named, is the direct creator and source of all the things in the world, just as a mother is the direct creator and source of the child.[126] This means there are two aspects of the Tao. One is the transcendent and purely ontological aspect, which is an ontological absolute and the ultimate support of each and everything. This may be termed the higher Tao. The other aspect of Tao is that which apparently acts as the direct creator and immediate source of all phenomenal entities. It manifests itself and seems to act in the context of all phenomenal parameters such as space, time,

---

124 Legge, James, Tr. *Tao-Teh-Ching,* 1-1, www.FreeSpiritualEbooks.com, 2008.

125 Legge, James, Tr. *Tao-Teh-Ching,* 1-2, www.FreeSpiritualEbooks.com, 2008.

126 Legge, James, Tr. *Tao-Teh-Ching,* 1-2, www.FreeSpiritualEbooks.com, 2008.

causality, reason and language. As such, it has been referred to as the Mother of all things. Tao-Teh-Ching further talks about the importance of desire lessness in the context of Tao and points out that it is imperative to be completely free of all desires to intuit the real nature of Tao.[127] If one is still tainted with even the slightest desire, then only the peripheral nature of Tao will be understood. This obstructive effect of desire with respect to the knowledge of Tao will be discussed in detail later in the Tao-Teh-Ching. These two aspects of the Tao are ontologically identical, but they are referred to by different names only due to the course of epistemic creation making it amenable to the phenomenal parameters such as space, time, causality, reason and language.[128] Taking both the aspects of Tao together, it may be simply called the Mystery, since the comprehension of its real nature is actually beyond the range of reason and language.

Tao-Teh-Ching beautifully discusses the reason for the futility of reason and language in handling the nature of the Tao. It points out that whenever we think about any concept or say a particular term representing some concept or entity, it is logically implicit that we understand its distinction from its opposite concept or its opposite term.[129] That is to say, the use of reason and language necessarily implies the presupposition of dualities, which ultimately indicates the realm of pluralities. But, the ontological nature of Tao is that of an absolute i.e. there is nothing other than that. In such a scenario, there can

---

[127] Legge, James, Tr. *Tao-Teh-Ching,* 1-3, www.FreeSpiritualEbooks.com, 2008.

[128] Legge, James, Tr. *Tao-Teh-Ching,* 1-4, www.FreeSpiritualEbooks.com, 2008.

[129] Legge, James, Tr. *Tao-Teh-Ching,* 2-2, www.FreeSpiritualEbooks.com, 2008.

be no possibility of the use of reason and language for grasping the nature of Tao. Therefore, the Tao realized sages do not take the help of speech for giving instructions about the nature of Tao.[130] Everything springs from the transcendent Tao, yet no one understands how it all happens. The Tao never shows itself as the source and creator of everything; yet everything gets accomplished ultimately due to the Tao alone.[131] It is this humble and mysterious nature of the Tao that makes it the supreme reality that it is.

Tao-Teh-Ching compares Tao with the emptiness of a vessel and points out that in order to understand the nature of Tao, one needs to empty oneself and constantly be on guard against fullness.[132] The term *hsu* is used for emptiness in Chinese. The higher Tao has also been called *Wu,* which means nothingness. Wu does not stand for absolute nothingness; instead, it stands for no-thingness, i.e. the lack of all phenomenal things. So, in the higher Tao there is no possibility of any phenomenal entity. Therefore, for intuiting the nature of Tao, one needs to rid oneself of all phenomenal ideas and desires. Only when the mind and heart is devoid of all worldly desires, there can be the understanding of the Tao. Hence, the higher Tao is also known as Wu, as a consequence of its transcendent nature. Further, the spiritual discipline of cultivating the state of emptiness or hsu becomes the path of realizing the Tao. With reference to its transcendent nature, Tao-Teh-Ching says one does not know whose son is the

---

[130] Legge, James, Tr. *Tao-Teh-Ching,* 2-3, www.FreeSpiritualEbooks.com, 2008.

[131] Legge, James, Tr. *Tao-Teh-Ching,* 2-4, www.FreeSpiritualEbooks.com, 2008.

[132] Legge, James, Tr. *Tao-Teh-Ching,* 4-1, www.FreeSpiritualEbooks.com, 2008.

higher Tao.[133] That is to say, there is no further ontological ground of the higher Tao. It is itself the supreme ontological ground. Not only this, the higher Tao seems to be preceding even God, the creator and sustainer of the world, both ontologically and chronologically. That is to say, God, as the lower aspect and manifestation of Tao, is itself ontologically grounded in the higher Tao.

Due to its transcendent nature, the higher Tao is referred to as the *Unnameable* and the lower aspect of the Tao is referred to as the *Nameable.* The phenomenal parameters of space, time, causality, reason and language apply only to the lower Tao, not to the transcendent higher Tao. For the same reason, the higher Tao is also known as *Wu* or *Nothingness,* and the lower Tao is known as *Being*. However, it should always be borne in mind that these are only two *aspects* of the Tao and not two Taos. The difference is only epistemic in nature and in terms of the transcendence of or the application of the phenomenal categories. It is somewhat analogous to the two states of the same ocean - one, when it is completely placid and the other, when it is full of waves and currents.

Heaven and earth, i.e. God seems to be benevolent towards all entities in the world, but Tao-Teh-Ching says that God does not act benevolently in a deliberate manner; God treats all phenomenal entities in an equal and ordinary manner, but it is also a fact that the activities of God definitely appear to be benevolent towards one and all.[134] In a similar manner, the sages *(sheng)* seem to be benevolent towards all

---

133 Legge, James, Tr. *Tao-Teh-Ching,* 4-3, www.FreeSpiritualEbooks.com, 2008.

134 Legge, James, Tr. *Tao-Teh-Ching,* 5-1, www.FreeSpiritualEbooks.com, 2008.

beings, but they do not act so in a deliberate manner; rather, they treat all in an equal manner and do not consider anyone as special.[135] This particular passage from the Tao-Teh-Ching highlights another important point also. That which is the nature of the Tao, gets naturally reflected in the nature and behaviour of the Tao realized sages. So, benevolent activity on the part of both Tao, as God, and the sages, is not a matter of deliberate choice; instead, it is a matter of inherent natural behaviour. The realization of the Tao by the sages changes them absolutely. They get attuned to the nature of the Tao and behave similarly in a natural manner.

Tao-Teh-Ching calls the source of the heaven and earth as the *female mystery* and the *root.*[136] This female mystery or the root refers to that aspect of the Tao which manifests itself as amenable to the various phenomenal parameters. This aspect is surely distinct from the transcendent aspect of the Tao, but not ontologically. They are distinct only in terms of manifestation. One should never forget the fact that the ontological framework of Taoism is an absolutist one, which means there is one and only one existential reality and that is the Tao. Now, this female mystery and the root is the source and therefore, the creator of the world, which means it is what we commonly refer to as God. This passage further sheds light on the nature of its functioning by pointing out that it has been eternally functioning so, in a smooth and natural manner, without any exertion and pain. That is to say, the creative function belongs naturally and eternally to the lower aspect of the Tao. This lower aspect of Tao is the God of Taoism and it

---

[135] Legge, James, Tr. *Tao-Teh-Ching,* 5-1, www.FreeSpiritualEbooks.com, 2008.

[136] Legge, James, Tr. *Tao-Teh-Ching,* 6, www.FreeSpiritualEbooks.com, 2008.

is also referred to as Teh. There are various other connotations of Teh as well, but being God or the lower and manifest aspect of the Tao is one of its primary connotations.

Further, Tao-Teh-Ching points out the reasons for the longevity of the earth and heaven, that is, the world, and relates those reasons with the enduring and fulfilling nature of the Tao realized saint. Two such reasons have been given. The first one is that the world is rooted in the Tao and thus springs from it and other one is that it does not live for itself, but for the Tao, as its ultimate destiny.[137] These reasons apply in the case of the Tao realized saint as well, in the sense that the saint is rooted in his intuitive realization of the Tao. His whole personality springs from that Tao realization. Further, all his activities are devoted to the Tao only. He never aims for his own preservation, yet he is always fully preserved and all his personal needs are fulfilled.[138]

Tao-Teh-Ching points out the similarity between the nature of water and that of Tao and presents this similarity as the highest excellence.[139] Water has the nature of nourishing all lives and benefiting all. It never strives to occupy a high position. On the contrary, it has the nature of occupying the lowest place available to it in a humble manner. This nature of water is comparable to the highest moral excellence and this excellence is reflective of and comparable to the nature of Tao as well, because the Tao sustains all, without ever showing

---

137 Legge, James, Tr. *Tao-Teh-Ching,* 7-1, www.FreeSpiritualEbooks.com, 2008.

138 Legge, James, Tr. *Tao-Teh-Ching,* 7-2, www.FreeSpiritualEbooks.com, 2008.

139 Legge, James, Tr. *Tao-Teh-Ching,* 8-1, www.FreeSpiritualEbooks.com, 2008.

itself as the supreme entity, and it benefits all, without any distinction whatsoever. The text further talks about the *mysterious quality* of the Tao, wherein it says that although the Tao is the creator and sustainer of the entire world, yet it never tries to show itself as such.[140] It never shows itself as the source of everything. Its true nature is revealed to someone only after untiring sustained efforts in that direction. Although it presides over each and everything, yet it provides them the freedom to choose their own courses. Despite its omnipotence, it does not try to control anything. This excellence itself is the 'mysterious quality' of the Tao. This mysterious quality is representative of the humility and ego lessness of the Tao.

Tao-Teh-Ching further points out the value and usefulness of emptiness (hsu) and thereby it also shows the higher and basic value of the higher Tao or Wu.[141] It gives the analogy of the emptiness of wheel, because of which the spokes become useful. If the wheel did not have emptiness between the spokes, the wheel would have lost its usefulness due to the heavy weight of the wheel. Similarly, the usefulness of a clay vessel or any vessel per se, is because of its emptiness. It is the empty space of the vessel which provides it the containing capacity, without which it would be totally useless. Further, the emptiness of house within its walls provides it usefulness. If the house becomes all full and solid, it would lose its value altogether. Further, the emptiness of the walls in its windows and door, make it useful. Without its windows and door, it would rather become an obstruction. Therefore, the things which have a positive existence, have their utility

---

[140] Legge, James, Tr. *Tao-Teh-Ching,* 10-3, www.FreeSpiritualEbooks.com, 2008.

[141] Legge, James, Tr. *Tao-Teh-Ching,* 11, www.FreeSpiritualEbooks.com, 2008.

through their adaptability and flexibility. But, this adaptability and flexibility itself is possible because of the non-existence or absence or voidness of some critical spaces. Therefore, the value of emptiness lies in the fact that it provides the positively existent entities the necessary space for adaptability and flexibility, which ultimately renders them useful and valuable. Similarly, it is the nothingness or non-existence or Wu of the higher Tao which makes possible the manifestation and value of the lower Tao or Being, which then becomes capable of acting as the creator, sustainer and destroyer of the world. Thus, even though there is no particular or phenomenal existence in the higher Tao, yet without its invisible and incomprehensible ontological support, nothing whatsoever can come to have a positive existence.

Tao-Teh-Ching indicates the transcendent qualities of the higher Tao by saying that it beyond the grasp of our eyes, ears and the mind.[142] Hence, it is said to be invisible, inaudible and subtle. These are all negative indications of the nature of the higher Tao. Combining together these negative indications one may try to vaguely indicate the nature of the higher Tao, which is, truly speaking, beyond all descriptions. Thus, Tao-Teh-Ching shows that the higher Tao can only be negatively indicated, as it is beyond all positive descriptions. With reference to the nature of Tao, Tao-Teh-Ching further elaborates its nature and says that its upper part i.e. the higher Tao is not bright. That is, the higher Tao is not visible and comprehensible. But its lower part is not obscure i.e. the lower Tao is not invisible and incomprehensible.[143] It is within the

---

[142] Legge, James, Tr. *Tao-Teh-Ching,* 14-1, www.FreeSpiritualEbooks.com, 2008.

[143] Legge, James, Tr. *Tao-Teh-Ching,* 14-2, www.FreeSpiritualEbooks.com, 2008.

framework of phenomenal parameters i.e. it can be grasped through space, time, causality, reason and language. This Tao acts ceaselessly, manifesting its lower aspect and creating the world through it. It also withdraws everything back into its transcendent void, including the manifestation of the lower Tao. But, despite all this, it cannot be given a name, as it is transcendent in nature; beyond the range of language and reason. Tao-Teh-Ching refers to this as the *form of the formless* and the *semblance of the invisible.* That is to say, the form and appearance of the formless and invisible higher Tao can be grasped in this manner only. The text goes on to say that in our daily phenomenal lives we are actually always following the Tao only, yet we do not realize it as such.[144] When we become capable of living our phenomenal lives in accordance with the nature of the pristine Tao i.e. the higher Tao, then one finds the clue to the nature of the higher Tao. That is to say, only by moulding our thoughts and behaviour in accordance with the nature of the higher Tao, we come closer to the inner realization of higher Tao at the intuitive plane.

The state of emptiness (hsu) should be cultivated with utmost care. That is, one should strive hard to free oneself from all worldly and selfish desires. Also, the stillness of the mind and breath should be constantly practised.[145] This constant and careful practice leads one to realize the unfailing law of reversion or *fan.* This law of reversion ensures that everything in this cosmos goes through a cycle, in which after reaching its climax it reverts back to its root, from where it had originated. The returning to its root is called the state of stillness and this

---

144 Legge, James, Tr. *Tao-Teh-Ching,* 14-3, www.FreeSpiritualEbooks.com, 2008.

145 Legge, James, Tr. *Tao-Teh-Ching,* 16-1, www.FreeSpiritualEbooks.com, 2008.

state of stillness reports the realization and fulfilment of the final destiny of that entity. The reporting of the fulfilment of the final destiny is the unfailing law of reversion. The persons who understand the unfailing nature of the law of reversion are said to be spiritually enlightened and they are possessed of the Tao.[146] Being possessed of the Tao, they become free from the danger of decay throughout their phenomenal lives. This law of reversion is the direct phenomenal manifestation of the nature of Tao. Hence, understanding this law immediately leads to an understanding of the Tao. The logical implication of this law is that each and every entity in this world is going through a cyclic process, in which the final destination is the starting point itself. Therefore, nothing can retain its nature forever. Everything is necessarily going through changes. This very realization stops one from getting attached to worldly states and entities, which thereby leads to the cessation of worldly desires. Moreover, the ultimate ontological ground of everything is the higher Tao; hence, all worldly manifestations, including the lower Tao itself, must fulfil their ultimate destiny by merging back into that transcendent higher Tao. Thus, the proper understanding of the law of reversion gives one the knowledge that the ultimate source and ground of everything is the higher Tao, from which and in which everything seems to manifest itself, and into which everything is destined to merge back. This spiritual realization enables one to see everything as a play and manifestation of the Tao itself. As a result of such realization, one's ego and worldly desires get eliminated completely and that sage becomes possessed of the Tao. Being possessed of the Tao, he

---

[146] Legge, James, Tr. *Tao-Teh-Ching,* 16-2, www.FreeSpiritualEbooks.com, 2008.

is no longer bound by worldly fears and aspirations related to his mortal physical frame.

Tao-Teh-Ching points out some of the bewildering characteristics of the Tao. To begin with, it says that the Tao is the source of the grandest active force, where this force is to be understood as the lower Tao i.e. Teh or God.[147] Teh or God is the greatest active force in the phenomenal universe because it is the creator, sustainer and destroyer of the world. It is impossible to describe the nature of the Tao as it is beyond the grasp of our senses and mind. Yet, in that higher Tao itself all the forms of the potential entities of the cosmos lie latent. Although it is itself formless and transcendent, yet it latently contains all possible forms of potential entities. The nature of Tao is mysterious and unfathomable. It cannot be given any name but it retains its essential nature in the transcendent realm, which lies beyond space, time, causality, language and reason. In its transcendent aspect, the Tao never faces any change or corruption. It remains immutable ontologically. Further, since all phenomenal forms and entities are ultimately grounded in the Tao itself, therefore everything, in their ontological essence, is but one with that transcendent Tao. The Tao realized sage sees the Tao only in all the entities of the world. He does not get deluded by their passing appearance and characteristics. Instead, he focuses his attention on the ontological essence of all those entities and finds everywhere the Tao alone. Thus, for the Tao realized sage, the fleeting world of changes is only the outer appearance, to which he does not give any importance. He gives importance only to the

---

147 Legge, James, Tr. *Tao-Teh-Ching*, 21, www.FreeSpiritualEbooks.com, 2008.

unchanging and transcendent ontological essence of everything, which is but identical with the Tao.

Tao-Teh-Ching talks of some aspects of the source of heaven and earth. Heaven stands for all the celestial bodies taken together, while earth refers to all the mundane entities. So, heaven and earth taken together represents the entire cosmos. Now, the source of this heaven and earth is indicated as formless and perfectly still, yet it acts as the source of all things with form.[148] This source of all is beyond all changes and omnipresent. It is beyond all decay. As it is the source of all, it may be called the *Mother* of all things. This may also be called the Tao.[149] It actually refers to the lower aspect of the Tao. This is also called the Teh and since it acts as the source of all, therefore it has also been called the *Great*. This Teh, the lower Tao or the Great, manifests itself as the world of plurality through the parameters of space, time, causality, reason and language. Having manifested itself thus, it apparently moves away from its original formless and still form and after reaching the climax of this remote manifestation, it comes back to merge into its original root, namely the Teh.[150] The unmanifest state of this Teh is ontologically identical with the higher Tao. The state of lower Tao i.e. Teh, becomes significant only when it gets involved in the act of manifesting the heaven and earth. Thus, the Tao is always in the process of manifesting and withdrawing itself in a cyclical manner. Ontologically, it is always immutable, but

---

148 Legge, James, Tr. *Tao-Teh-Ching,* 25-1, www.FreeSpiritualEbooks.com, 2008.

149 Legge, James, Tr. *Tao-Teh-Ching,* 25-2, www.FreeSpiritualEbooks.com, 2008.

150 Legge, James, Tr. *Tao-Teh-Ching,* 25-3, www.FreeSpiritualEbooks.com, 2008.

epistemically, it is always undergoing manifestation and withdrawal. Therefore, its transcendence and immanence are maintained simultaneously. The simultaneity of its transcendence and immanence is logically puzzling and it has not been elaborated in the Tao-Teh-Ching, but Chuang-Tzu, a leading disciple of Lao-Tze, has tried to explain it in his book. Tao-Teh-Ching further tells us about the law of the Tao and says that it basically springs from its own nature.[151] That is, the entire phenomenal cosmos and all its laws are just a manifestation of the Tao and its nature. Everything in this world is nothing but a manifestation of the Tao.

The two aspects of the Tao and their relationship with the world have been clearly depicted in the Tao-Teh-Ching. The Tao, in its transcendent and immutable ontological nature, cannot be named.[152] It is the *Unnameable*. But, as soon as it gets into the mode of manifesting itself as the cosmos, it has a name and hence, it is referred to as the *Nameable Tao*. In this aspect as Teh, it is the God and people can take refuge in it. Taking refuge in this Teh, people become morally and spiritually perfect and free from failure and error.[153] Thus, the Nameable and the Unnameable Tao are ontologically identical. Their aspects differ only in terms of their absolute transcendence and manifesting activity. The nature of relationship existing between the Teh and the worldly entities has been depicted as comparable to the relationship that exists between the great rivers and ocean and the infinite number of streams and

---

[151] Legge, James, Tr. *Tao-Teh-Ching,* 25-4, www.FreeSpiritualEbooks.com, 2008.

[152] Legge, James, Tr. *Tao-Teh-Ching,* 32-1, www.FreeSpiritualEbooks.com, 2008.

[153] Legge, James, Tr. *Tao-Teh-Ching,* 32-4, www.FreeSpiritualEbooks.com, 2008.

rivulets running down the valleys and mountains.[154] That is to say, the totality of all phenomenal entities constitutes the manifest form of the Teh. It is thus immanent in all the entities of the world.

The great Tao is all pervading. There is no corner in the cosmos where the Tao does not exist.[155] All entities ultimately derive their existence from the Tao only and everything obeys the laws and directions of the Tao. It is immanent in each and every entity; hence, it may be named in the smallest thing as well as in the greatest thing.[156] Thus, everything in its totality is nothing but the manifestation of the Tao and each individual entity in itself is also the Tao. The Tao, being transcendent, does not do anything for the sake of doing it. That is, it does not have any aim or objective to achieve. Yet, it gets involved in the activity of manifesting itself as the world. Then, why does it do it? It does not manifest it for the sake of manifesting it; rather, this manifestation takes place due to its inherent nature.[157] In this manner, one the one hand, the Tao does not do anything intentionally and deliberately; on the other hand, whatever is done in the world, is done only because of the Tao. The manifesting act of the Tao proceeds through contraries i.e. in terms of contrasting dualities.[158] The whole phenomenal world manifests through infinite number of contrasting

---

[154] Legge, James, Tr. *Tao-Teh-Ching,* 32-5, www.FreeSpiritualEbooks.com, 2008.

[155] Legge, James, Tr. *Tao-Teh-Ching,* 34-1, www.FreeSpiritualEbooks.com, 2008.

[156] Legge, James, Tr. *Tao-Teh-Ching,* 34-2, www.FreeSpiritualEbooks.com, 2008.

[157] Legge, James, Tr. *Tao-Teh-Ching,* 37-1, www.FreeSpiritualEbooks.com, 2008.

[158] Legge, James, Tr. *Tao-Teh-Ching,* 40-1, www.FreeSpiritualEbooks.com, 2008.

dualities and this manifestation takes place in a natural and subtle manner, in which no force seems to be used. All existing entities i.e. the whole phenomenal world came into existence from the Non-existence. That is, existence sprang out of Non-existence.[159] That is to say, the existent and nameable is a manifestation of the non-existence and unnameable. The lower Tao or Teh is a manifestation of the higher Tao or Wu.

The higher Tao is intangible, invisible, unnameable and transcendent, yet it is that alone from which everything springs and that alone which looks after the needs of everything and makes them complete.[160] Tao, in its lower aspect as Teh or God, looks after the needs of each and every entity in the world and fulfilling their requirements, makes them complete. Not only that, it is this Teh alone which subtly guides each and every entity towards its ultimate destiny, namely the Tao itself. The mysterious operation of the Tao consists in the fact that even though it is the source and sustainer of all entities in the world, as well as the ultimate controller of all entities, yet it never shows off itself as such and provides each entity the freedom to act in accordance with its nature.[161] This shows the innate humility of the Tao.

That aspect of the Tao from which everything sprang up, may be called the Mother of all things and this aspect of the Tao is known as Teh or God.[162] Once the nature of the source

---

[159] Legge, James, Tr. *Tao-Teh-Ching,* 40-2, www.FreeSpiritualEbooks.com, 2008.

[160] Legge, James, Tr. *Tao-Teh-Ching,* 41-3, www.FreeSpiritualEbooks.com, 2008.

[161] Legge, James, Tr. *Tao-Teh-Ching,* 51-3,4, www.FreeSpiritualEbooks.com, 2008.

[162] Legge, James, Tr. *Tao-Teh-Ching,* 52-1, www.FreeSpiritualEbooks.com, 2008.

or Mother is understood, one can easily understand what ought to be the ideal characteristics in that Mother's children. If the characteristics of the Mother are guarded and cultivated in the children, then there will be no fear and failure for them.[163] The sage who really knows the Tao, does not care to speak about it as he is fully aware of its transcendent nature, but the person who is ever ready to speak about the nature of the Tao, surely has not grasped the true nature of the Tao.[164]

3.2 The Dynamics of Tao and Teh

In the previous section various aspects of the metaphysics of Tao have been discussed in the light of Tao-Teh-Ching. We have seen that there are two aspects of the Tao - the higher and the lower Tao, which are also known as Tao and Teh, or Wu and the Mother of all things, or non-existence and being, or the transcendent Tao and the immanent Tao, or Nothingness and God respectively. Further, various characteristics of these twin aspects of the Tao have been described in the Tao-Teh-Ching. However, many of these characteristics seem to conflicting in their nature and implications. These apparently conflicting characteristics have not been resolved in a compatible manner in the Tao-Teh-Ching. This task was left to the Chuang-Tzu, the leading disciple of Lao-Tze, who authored the Chuang-Tzu book. Chuang-Tzu's comprehension of the dynamics of Tao shall also be discussed in this section, but let us first take a look at the prominent characteristics of the twin aspects of the Tao, along with the conflicts arising from them.

---

163 Legge, James, Tr. *Tao-Teh-Ching,* 52-2, www.FreeSpiritualEbooks.com, 2008.

164 Legge, James, Tr. *Tao-Teh-Ching,* 56-1, www.FreeSpiritualEbooks.com, 2008.

To begin with, it has been clearly mentioned repeatedly in the Tao-Teh-Ching that the Tao is the only reality. There is nothing apart from the Tao. Philosophically, this means the ontological framework of Taoism is absolutist in nature. Further, the text refers to Tao as the immutable reality, which means the Tao does not suffer from changes. It has also been mentioned clearly that in one aspect, the Tao is purely transcendent to all the phenomenal categories, whereas in the other aspect it is the source and Mother of heaven and earth. It is the Mother of all things. Thus, Tao is both transcendent and immanent at the same time. It is said that the Tao creates, sustains and withdraws back the whole world.

The above-mentioned description of the Tao throws up many conflicting situations about the nature of the Tao, which demand a logically consistent resolution. Let us take a look at some of these problems. Firstly, if Tao is the sole ontological absolute, then how is plurality of the world to be explained? Secondly, if Tao is an immutable reality, then how can the creation of the world be explained out of it? Thirdly, how can the Tao be both immanent and transcendent simultaneously? Fourthly, if Tao is immutable, then what could be the nature of changes associated with the creation, sustenance and withdrawal of all the phenomenal entities. Lastly, how could the immutable Tao be associated with *fan* or the law of reversion, as a manifestation of its inherent nature?

In order to arrive at the possible answers to these puzzling questions, we first need to understand how Chuang-Tzu understands the nature and dynamics of the Tao. We can try to grasp his outlook with the help of an analogy, which is the ocean and its waves. However, one has to be careful in not stretching the analogy too far, otherwise it would fail to serve its purpose. No phenomenal analogy can ever be perfect for explaining the nature and dynamics of the transcendent reality. Therefore, one has to be careful in using the analogy for trying to understand the nature of the transcendent reality. One can think of the ocean as one unchanging entity, in the sense that its huge mass of water always remains the same. That is, no change takes place in the overall nature of the ocean. Yet, within the ocean itself, there are huge number of waves that keep on rising and falling all the time. The same mass of water sometimes remains placid, but at other times that very mass of water takes up the shape of a wave, without adding to or reducing from that mass of water. The crest and trough of a wave are carved out of the same mass of water through the internal dynamics of the ocean. Therefore, when the crest and trough of the wave move back to their starting point, they mutually cancel out each other's manifestation and then only the level placid water of the ocean remains. These internal dynamics of the ocean to continually manifest itself in the form of waves and revert back to its placid state, is the inherent nature of the ocean and it does not add to or reduce from the overall mass of water constituting the ocean.

On similar lines, Chuang-Tzu thinks of the Tao as one absolute transcendent entity, which is immutable, because there is no possibility of any genuine addition or reduction from its constituent ontological reality. Yet, due to its inherent internal nature and dynamics, an internal redistribution of its ontological constituent reality keeps taking place continually. Such redistribution leads to the manifestation of various phenomenal parameters such as space, time, causality, reason and language, as well as various phenomenal entities in due course. This redistribution is neither permanent nor unidirectional. It is temporary and cyclical. That is, the redistributions which manifest the phenomenal entities and their parameters, subside and merge back into their starting points after a while, leading to that state of the Tao which is free from all phenomenal parameters and thus transcendent. So, one can see here that ultimately speaking, no change takes place in the overall ontological constitution of the Tao. Therefore, the absoluteness and immutability of the Tao becomes evident. Further, whatever redistributive manifestations take place within the Tao, they are all constituted within the Tao itself and also constituted by the ontological stuff of the Tao. Therefore, all the manifested phenomenal entities are firmly grounded in the Tao alone and the Tao is always immanent in all of them. So, the omnipresence and immanence of the Tao in the whole phenomenal cosmos does not conflict with the overall absoluteness and transcendence of the Tao. Moreover, the redistributive phenomenal manifestations are not the result of any true ontological addition, deletion or modification of the constituent stuff of the Tao. As such, these modifications cannot be considered ontological in nature. Yet, since they are modifications nonetheless, therefore they can be treated as merely epistemic in nature. Further, the cyclic nature of these redistributive phenomenal manifestations cannot be attributed to anything other than the Tao, because the ontological absolutism of Tao does not allow the ontological possibility of anything apart from the Tao. As a result of this situation, the only logical implication left would suggest that it must be attributed to the inherent and inalienable nature of the Tao itself. Therefore, the law of reversion manifesting through all the phenomenal entities must be accepted as a reflective manifestation of the inherent nature of the Tao alone.

In this manner, Chuang-Tzu wonderfully sought to iron out the conflicting characteristics of the Tao. He showed the logical possibility of its simultaneous immutability and change, as well as its simultaneous transcendence and universal immanence. He also related the universally observable law of reversion with the inner nature of the Tao, and suggested indirectly the epistemic nature of all the phenomenal manifestations. Thus, the Tao-Chia of Lao-Tze and Chuang-Tzu presents a wonderful metaphysical framework, which explains and relates both the phenomenal world and the higher transcendent reality.

Chapter 4:
Spiritual Nature and Value of Niṣkāma-Karma

Bhagavadgītā represents the very essence of the entire Vedic tradition and amongst the various concepts and practices prescribed and highlighted by Bhagavadgītā, the concept of niṣkāma-karma or detached action occupied a pre-eminent position. In fact, niṣkāma-karma may be taken as the characteristic concept and teaching of Bhagavadgīta One may translate niṣkāma-karma as detached action, where detachment refers to the expected fruits or results of the action performed. Bhagavadgītā strongly propounds the theory that one should always perform all actions in a detached manner. The justifications for doing so have been elaborated in the Bhagavadgītā. But there are various aspects of the concept of niṣkāma-karma which need to be first properly understood before one may accept the worthiness of practising niṣkāma-karma. Not only does it present its worthiness to be practised as such, in fact Bhagavadgītā goes a step ahead and presents it as a universal duty that *ought* to be practised. The various justifications for presenting niṣkāma-karma as a universal duty are quite exhaustive and interesting, which shall be taken up in this chapter.

4.1 The Concept of Niṣkāma-Karma

The very term niṣkāma-karma stands for action that is devoid of desires. But, the question arises, desires for what? The answer is desires for the enjoying the anticipated fruits or results of the performed action. The very next question that comes up is why would anyone engage in an action if there is no desire for the enjoyment of its results. The common perception is that we engage in various actions for the sake of their expected results. So, it appears that if the desire for enjoying its result is not there, then no one would engage in any action. But we may look at the scenario from a slightly different angle as well. Any given person is always situated in some context of family, society, state, age, gender, etc. Associated with all these contextual situations, that person has to face various expectations and obligations related with his family, society, state, age, gender, etc. These expectations and obligations have a normative sense of *ought* attached with them. Hence, they define the duties of that person towards the family, society, state, humanity and the world at large.

Now, these duties are ordained by the person's given circumstances and situations. They do not take shape due to a willing desire on the part of that person. Our very birth in a family obliges us to perform certain duties and obligations towards our family members. Similarly, our very situation in a society and state obliges us to perform certain duties and obligations towards them. Our very existence as a human being obliges us to act in certain ways towards all humanity. Our very existence in this world obliges us to act in certain ways towards all entities in this world. Thus, there are various kinds and levels of duties that ought to be performed by a person, irrespective of his desire to engage with them. Thus, every person, irrespective of his personal desires, is necessarily obliged to perform various duties. Therefore, the superficial impression that if there is no personal desire for enjoying the anticipated results of an action, then no one would engage in any action, is a grossly misleading impression. On the contrary, the common man's life is mostly full of actions that constitute some sort of duty or the other. However, it is also a fact that the common man usually engages in those actions with an eye on the enjoyment of its anticipated results. So, the picture emerges that the common people mostly engage in various kinds of actions, as required by their circumstances, but they do it an attached manner, seeking to enjoy the anticipated results of those actions.

It is at this juncture that Bhagavadgītā points out the demerit of performing actions in an attached manner. Firstly, no one can ever have perfect control over the actual result of a performed action, as there are countless factors that play their roles in determining finally the actual outcome of that action. Secondly, the result of an action that goes against the expectations of the agent of that action, is bound to lead to a sense misery and disappointment. Thirdly and most importantly, irrespective of the nature of the result of the performed action, all attached actions are bound to bind karmically the agent of that action. So, in the spiritual and religious context, the performance of attached actions definitely leads to karmic bondage and spiritual ignorance. Now, the avowed aim of all religious-spiritual traditions is the attainment of spiritual knowledge and liberation, which amounts to an irreversible freedom from all phenomenal miseries and limitations. Bhagavadgītā declares in an emphatic manner that when an action is performed, purely out of a sense of duty, without any concern for its anticipated pleasant or unpleasant results, then that action does not have the potency to karmically bind the agent of that action. Further, the performance of one's duties in such a detached manner purifies one's mind and heart, which ultimately facilitates the eradication of spiritual ignorance, which in turn leads to the highest liberation.

Moreover, when a person engages in an action out of selfish motivations, then the reason for having such motivations is the deep-rooted spiritual ignorance regarding one's identity with the physical body. Thinking of oneself as being identical with the physical body is the fundamental form of spiritual ignorance, which is then responsible for the germination of various body related attachments and aversions. The attachment to anticipated pleasant results of actions and aversion to anticipated unpleasant results of actions, are therefore primarily grounded in the fundamental spiritual ignorance of bodily identification.

Therefore, the practice of performing one's duties, without any sense of attachment or aversion to the expected results of the action, amounts to hitting at the root cause of spiritual ignorance and bondage. When a person continuously performs only his obligatory duties, and that too only out of a pure sense of duty, then his sense of bodily identification automatically starts weakening. In due course, such practice of detached actions leads to the purification of the mind and heart, weakening the bonds of spiritual ignorance. Thus, the performance of one's duties in a completely detached manner is highly beneficial in the spiritual context.

But, what about the phenomenal aspects of performance of one's duties in a detached manner? It is an indubitable fact that despite one's best efforts there can be no guarantee about the actual result coming from an action. The actual result of any action depends on innumerable factors and most of those factors are beyond the control of the agent of that action. In such a scenario, performing any action for the sake of its anticipated result can surely be treated as credulous. Therefore, performing actions for the sake of enjoying the expected results of those actions can be treated as somewhat foolish. Further, if the result of the action leads to a pleasant result, then the agent gets further attached to the action and its result, leading him to perform such action repeatedly. But that action may not always give the same kind of result, and when it gives an unpleasant result, that person becomes miserable and disappointed. Moreover, an action may give an unpleasant result as well. In that situation, the person performing actions in an attached manner will surely be miserable and disappointed. This means, whether the performance of an attached action leads to a pleasant or unpleasant result, in both cases, the ultimate outcome is necessarily suffering, misery and disappointment. Moreover, not all necessary tasks in a family, society and state are always pleasant and desirable. Many essential tasks require patience, sacrifice and forbearing. Therefore, if all persons are guided only by the anticipated pleasantness of the result of the action, then many essential tasks would be left unattended, which would spell chaos and disaster for the family, society and the state. Therefore, even if one considers the performance of actions in a purely phenomenal context, it would be counter-productive if all persons perform actions only for the sake of their anticipated pleasant results. Thus, it can be seen that for both phenomenal and spiritual upliftment, it is desirable to perform one's duties purely out of a sense of duty, being totally detached to the anticipated results of those actions.

The continuous performance of one's duties in a completely detached manner, therefore, leads to phenomenal welfare as well as spiritual enlightenment and liberation. This path to spiritual enlightenment and liberation has been called the path of karma-yoga in Bhagavadgītā. Karma-yoga may be translated as the path of action, leading to union with the supreme reality. More specifically, it may be called the path of detached actions leading to the union with the supreme reality. Karma-yoga is one of the three important paths to liberation, according to the Bhagavadgītā. The other two paths to liberation are Jñāna-yoga and Bhakti-yoga. Jñāna-yoga is the path to liberation through spiritual knowledge. It has also been referred to as Sāṅkhya-yoga in the Bhagavadgītā, as Sāṅkhya literally means proper knowledge. Bhakti-yoga is the path to liberation through devotion to God. It is important to note that in the light of the Bhagavadgītā, these three paths to liberation cannot be rigidly distinguished from each other. On the contrary, they are rather inter-dependent and even presume each other to some extent. These three paths correspond with the cognitive, conative and emotive faculties of a human being. All three paths lead to the same divine goal, but it is the aptitude of a given person that is critical in deciding the suitability of a particular path for that person. Every person has all the three faculties and operates through them in the phenomenal world. However, the cognitive faculty may be dominant in some person, while the conative or emotive faculty may be dominating in the case of other persons. Therefore, Jñāna-yoga would be the suitable spiritual path for a person with a predominant intellectual and cognitive faculty. Bhakti-yoga would be suitable for a person with a predominant emotive faculty and Karma-yoga would be suitable for the ordinary person who is neither predominantly intellectual nor predominantly emotive. It thus emerges that for the vast majority of humans, karma-yoga turns out to be the suitable spiritual path, which caters to both phenomenal and spiritual fulfilment.

Now, let us take a look at some of the representative passages from the Bhagavadgītā which discuss the various aspects of karma-yoga and niṣkāma-karma, as well as about the characteristics of the perfected karma-yogī. The absolute worthiness of one's righteous duty has been categorically emphasized by the Bhagavadgītā.[165] That is, the duties ordained by one's family, society, state and stage of life, ought to be carried out with utmost respect and sincerity. One should never neglect one's duties. Further, neglecting one's righteous duties leads to defamation and demerit, i.e. it causes both phenomenal and spiritual degradation.[166] Hence, from both perspectives, one should never neglect one's duties. Remaining even minded in the face of pleasure and pain, victory and loss, resulting from the performance of one's righteous duties renders one free from all possible demerits.[167] That is, performing one's duties with complete detachment to the anticipated results of those actions, makes one free from all possibilities of demerits and karmic bondage. Another significant aspect of karma-yoga is that even a little practice of this discipline never goes waste and one starts form the point where it had been left, whether in the present life or the future life.[168] That is, the practice of karma-yoga can be perfected through many phenomenal lives, if required.

In the most famous passage related to Karma-yoga, Bhagavadgītā declares that a person's jurisdiction is limited to the performance of one's righteous duties and actions and it does not ever spread over to the results of those actions.[169] One should never act as a means for the result of an action. One

---

165 Bhagavadgītā, 2-31.

166 Bhagavadgītā, 2-33.

167 Bhagavadgītā, 2-38.

168 Bhagavadgītā, 2-40.

169 *karmaṇyevādhikāraste mā phaleṣu kadācana,*
mā karmaphalaheturbhūrmā te saṅgo'stvakarmaṇi, Bhagavadgītā, 2-47.

should also not become attached to inactivity. That is to say, one should perform one's duties only out of a sense of duty and never for the sake of its result. At the same time, one should vigorously perform one's duties and beware of attachment to inactivity. Thus, the practice of karma-yoga consists in the performance of niṣkāma-karma. When a person chooses to perform detached actions, his activities will automatically get restricted to his duties alone. Therefore, niṣkāma-karma implies the performance of one's duties in a completely detached manner. Yoga consists in remaining completely indifferent to the success or failure resulting from the performance of one's duties. Retaining one's poise and being even minded in the face of all possible eventualities is known as yoga or union with the higher reality.[170] That is, if a person remains equipoised in all situations, while performing one's duties, his mind and heart get purified to such an extent that he attains the highest spiritual knowledge and liberation.

A person carrying out his duties in the spirit of niṣkāma-karma transcends both karmic merit and demerit even while living in this phenomenal world. The skill of performing one's duties in the spirit of niṣkāma-karma is the highest skill of performing actions and this is referred to as Yoga or union with the highest reality.[171] It is an indisputable fact that as long as person is alive, he will continue to perform one function or the other. Even if one tries not to do anything, at least the person will keep breathing, seeing, hearing, thinking, etc. Therefore, complete abstention from actions is practically impossible and ordinary actions definitely bind a person karmically. As such, performing actions as niṣkāma-karma so

---

170 ...*samatvaṁ yoga ucyate,* Bhagavadgītā, 2-48.

171 ...*yogaḥ karmasu kauśalam,* Bhagavadgītā, 2-50.

that they no longer bind one karmically, is declared as the highest skill and dexterity in the performance of actions. Such detached actions lead to the realization of the highest spiritual realization and its resultant liberation.[172] That is why karma-yoga is an important path to liberation. Now, what are the characteristics of a person who has mastered the art of performing detached actions? Such a person is declared to have attained the highest spiritual realization and liberation. Hence, the characteristics of a karma-yogī *par excellence* are also the characteristics of a spiritually realized and liberated while alive person. Such a person's thoughts and convictions are fully stabilized in the highest spiritual knowledge and realization.

Such a spiritually perfected person is referred to as a *sthitaprajña,* that is, a person whose intellect and convictions are fully grounded in the highest spiritual knowledge. When a person has rid his mind and heart of all worldly desires and he is completely satisfied with his own inner spiritual nature and being, then that person can validly be called a *sthitaprajña.*[173] Such a spiritual master is also a karma-yogī *par excellence.* Such a person does not get perturbed by the experiences of misery and pain, and he also does not feel elated in the experiences of pleasures. He has transcended the emotions of attachment, fear and anger and hence, his mind is said to be fully stabilized in spiritual wisdom.[174] Such a person has transcended all attachments. Therefore, when he comes across pleasant and unpleasant experiences, neither does he

---

[172] *...padaṁ gacchanty-anāmayam, Bhagavadgītā,* 2-51.

[173] *prajahāti yadā kāmān-sarvān-pārtha manogatān,*
ātmanyevātmanā tuṣṭaḥ sthitaprajñas-tadocyate, Bhagavadgītā, 2-55.

[174] *...vīta-rāga-bhaya-krodaḥ sthitadhīra-munir-ucyate,* Bhagavadgītā, 2-56.

welcome those experiences, nor does he feel averse to them. Such equanimous state of mind belongs only to the spiritually perfected person, a perfected karma-yogī, a *sthitaprajña*.[175] Just as a tortoise can withdraw all its limbs inside and cut off itself from the outside world, similarly the *sthitaprajña* person can withdraw all of his senses from their respective sense objects and remain unperturbed by the outside world.[176] This withdrawal and internalization of the sense organs has also been referred to as *pratyāhāra,* the fifth limb of the eight limbed yoga of Patañjalī. This is a necessary step for further higher yogic practices because unless the mind is free from its external engagements with the various sense objects, the internal focus of consciousness cannot be realized.

Although it is true that the withdrawal of all the senses from their respective sense objects is a necessary precondition for the higher yogic disciplines, yet the fact remains that for the spiritual aspirant this withdrawal is a willing and deliberate process, which implies that he may still be having the inner impressions of the various sense experiences lingering in his mind. As long as spiritual perfection is not realized, these subtle impressions do linger on in the mind, but when the highest spiritual realization dawns on the aspirant he intuitively experiences the supreme bliss of Brahman and realizes it as his very own essential nature. Having experienced that supreme bliss of Brahman, the comparatively vastly inferior pleasures of the senses become insignificant and therefore, the perfected spiritual person, the *sthitaprajña,* becomes completely rid of all the subtle lingering impressions

---

175 …*nābhinandati na dveṣṭi tasya prajñā pratiṣṭhitā,* Bhagavadgītā, 2-57.

176 …*tasya prajñā pratiṣṭhitā,* Bhagavadgītā, 2-58.

of phenomenal sense pleasures.[177] The basic fact is that when a person has developed complete control over his senses, his intellect and mind get stabilized in the spiritual knowledge and wisdom, and this opens up the doors of spiritual realization.[178]

Bhagavadgītā presents a wonderful contrast between the spiritually perfected person, the perfect karma-yogī, the *sthitaprajña,* and the ordinary worldly persons. It says that which is night for the *sthitaprajña,* is day for the worldly people, and that which is day for the *sthitaprajña,* is night for the worldly people.[179] The idea is, that which is the realm of activities and aspirations for the worldly people, namely the phenomenal world, is something in which the perfected spiritual person is not very much interested. Although he is still active in the world, but he remains totally detached from the world and its experiences. On the contrary, that sphere in which the spiritual person is vigorously active and aspiring, namely the realm of spiritual knowledge and realization, is practically non-existent for the worldly people. So, the days and nights for the spiritual and the worldly people are mutually opposites. So, even though the karma-yogī remains vigorously active in the world, yet internally he remains detached from it and his sole area of interest and attention is the attainment of spiritual knowledge and liberation. With his mind totally engrossed in his spiritual ideal, yet performing his worldly duties in a detached manner, the perfect karma-yogī, the *sthitaprajña,* attains to the irreversible state of

---

177 *...rasavarjaṁ rasopyasya paraṁ dṛṣṭvā nivartate,* Bhagavadgītā, 2-59.

178 *...vaśe hi yasyendriyāṇi tasya prajñā pratiṣṭhitā,* Bhagavadgītā, 2-61.

179 *yā niśā sarva-bhūtānāṁ tasyāṁ jāgarti saṁyamī,*
yasyāṁ jāgrati bhūtāni sā niśā paśyato muneḥ, Bhagavadgītā, 2-69.

realizing one's perfect identity with Brahman and retaining this mental state, while leaving his mortal frame behind, he gets totally merged in that Brahman, the infinite bliss *par excellence.*

Bhagavadgītā points out that one cannot remain without doing any karma or activity, even for a moment, because all beings are constantly engaged in various kinds of actions under the influence of the three *guṇas* of Prakṛti.[180] Karma does not stand only for some external visible activity. Karma encompasses all those activities in which the sense of agency of the subject is involved, whether it physical, verbal or mental. If karma is understood as all that in which the sense of agency is involved, then it is obvious that as long as a person is alive, he cannot refrain from all activities or karmas. In such a situation, the adoption of karma-yoga or performing all activities in the detached spirit of niṣkāma-karma is the best way of overcoming the karmically binding effect of the karmas. In this way, the practice of karma-yoga is compatible with both the phenomenal and spiritual obligations, order and objectives. This is the unique quality and value of karma-yoga. A person who keeps performing his duties in a detached manner is a true karma-yogī and he excels in both the phenomenal and spiritual spheres.[181] Bhagavadgītā never advocates inactivity, because performing one's due obligations and duties is certainly better than not doing anything at all. Moreover, one's phenomenal needs and livelihood too cannot be fulfilled without the performance of karmas.[182]

---

[180] Bhagavadgītā, 3-5.

[181] *...karmendriyaiḥ karma-yogam-asaktaḥ sa viśiṣyate,* Bhagavadgītā, 3-7.

[182] Bhagavadgītā, 3-8.

Now, Bhagavadgītā relates the concept of *yajña* with the concept of niṣkāma-karma. It declares that only the karmas performed apart from those related to the *yajñas* are karmically binding in nature; therefore, one should engage only with the karmas related with the *yajñas.*[183] This passage is highly significant for understanding the nature and value of niṣkāma-karma. But first, we need to understand the meaning of *yajña* in the Vedic tradition. In the Vedic tradition, a *yajña* or ritual sacrifice is performed for the pleasure and strengthening of the Vedic *devas* or deities. Now, the Vedic deities represent the various kinds of natural forces working in the phenomenal world and they are the conscious entities controlling their respective jurisdictional natural forces. Vedic sacrifices also had the inherent motive of expressing one's gratitude to the deities for granting the world with various natural bounties, without which life would not have been possible. Thus, if one were to extract the basic significance of the *yajñas,* bereft of their religious and ritual aspects, it would be amply clear that the activities done for the strengthening and betterment of our given natural environment and ecology may be treated as the Vedic *yajñas.* Now, such Vedic sacrifices are never done for self-gratification or out of selfish motivations or for personally enjoying the anticipated results of those activities. They are done for the common good and welfare. That is, these *yajñas* are to be performed without having any personal attachment to their anticipated results, as a matter of duty and broader obligation. All this clearly shows that *yajñas* consist in performing our broader duties and obligations in a completely detached manner, which immediately shows the necessary

---

[183] *yajñārthāt-karmaṇo'nyatra loko'yaṁ karma-bandhanaḥ,*
tadarthaṁ karma kaunteya mukta-saṅgaḥ samācara, Bhagavadgītā, 3-9.

linkage between them and the niṣkāma-karma of Bhagavadgītā. It is in this light that one should understand the significance of the Bhagavadgītā passage which says that all actions performed apart from the *yajñas* are karmically binding in nature and hence one should abstain from doing anything other than the *yajñas.* Another very significant aspect of the *yajña* is pointed out in the succeeding passage wherein it is said that through the performance of the *yajñas,* the deities are satisfied and in turn, the deities fulfil the needs of the performer of the *yajñas.*[184] This passage indicates a deep and mysterious spiritual law. When a person works out of selfish motivations, for the sake of the anticipated results, then he has to face much uncertainty and even anxiety, depression and misery. But, when a person works with no attachment to the anticipated result of the action, for any selfish and personal enjoyment i.e. he works completely in the spirit of niṣkāma-karma, then the subtle spiritual powers ensure that his needs are properly fulfilled. So, the irony is that when one seeks and works for selfish gratification and enjoyment, there is always uncertainty attached with it, but when one does the same thing, not for the self but for the common good, his personal needs are well taken care of by the spiritual powers. So, the beauty of niṣkāma-karma is that by letting go the phenomenal selfish goals, one gains both the phenomenal and the spiritual goals.

Further ahead, Bhagavadgītā unequivocally exhorts all to follow the path of karma-yoga and niṣkāma-karma, because by practising it one attains the highest spiritual realization and liberation. The detached performance of one's duties and

---

[184] *devān-bhāvayatānena te devā bhāvayantu vaḥ,*
parasparaṁ bhāvayantaḥ śreyaḥ param-avāpsyatha, Bhagavadgītā, 3-11.

obligations have the great spiritual potential of granting one the highest realization and liberation.[185] The great significance of this statement from the Bhagavadgītā and that of niṣkāma-karma and karma-yoga, is that it presents a non-religious means of attaining the highest spiritual goal i.e. identity with Brahman and liberation. There is no essential religious or metaphysical prerequisite for the practice of niṣkāma-karma and karma-yoga. The skilful detached performance of one's duties and obligations, for the good of all, is by itself sufficient to ensure the realization of the highest spiritual objective, even though one may not be even aware of it or desiring it as such. However, it is also a fact that faith in the divine nature of God certainly goes a long way in facilitating the smooth practice of karma-yoga. Nonetheless, it would be no exaggeration to say that the Bhagavadgītā first of all propounded in the Vedic tradition a non-religious moral path to the highest spiritual realization and liberation. It is a pioneering contribution of the Bhagavadgītā. Moreover, without requiring any prior religious and metaphysical commitments, it presented a path to the fulfilment of both phenomenal wellbeing and spiritual realization and liberation. Bhagavadgītā goes ahead and cites the example of the sage king Janaka who had attained the highest realization of Brahman and was also widely respected for the efficient administration of his state. It was by resorting to the detached performance of his worldly duties and obligations alone that he had attained the highest spiritual knowledge.[186] Further, since the duties and obligations of any person are defined with respect to his situation in the family, society, state and the world at large, therefore all duties

---

[185] *tasmād-asaktaḥ satataṁ kāryaṁ karma samācara,*

askto hy-ācarana-karma param-āpnoti pūruṣaḥ, Bhagavadgītā, 3-19.

[186] *karmaṇaiva hi saṁsiddhim-āsthitā janakādayaḥ,* Bhagavadgītā, 3-20.

actually aim for the realization for the common good. This common good or welfare has been referred to as *loka-saṅgraha* in the Bhagavadgītā. Reluctance in the performance of one's duties and obligations harm the society more than oneself, because duties are meant to serve the common good and not our personal selfish whims. Therefore, keeping in view the common good or *loka-saṅgraha,* one ought to always perform one's prescribed duties and obligations.[187] Just as the worldly persons zealously perform various actions for the sake of their results in an attached manner, with a similar zeal should the spiritually enlightened ones go on performing their prescribed duties and obligations for the common good or *loka-saṅgraha,* in a completely detached manner.[188] Bhagavadgītā considers the performance of duties in an attached manner better than their non-performance, because, while their non-performance would adversely affect the common good or *loka-saṅgraha,* the attached performance would at least serve the common good, if not the personal spiritual upliftment of the agent of that action. Therefore, Bhagavadgītā clearly advises the spiritually enlightened persons to take care that the persons performing duties in an attached manner do not lapse into passivity and inactivity due to spiritual sermons.[189]

Talking about karma and akarma, actions and inactions respectively, Bhagavadgītā declares that one who can see action in inaction, and also inaction in action, is truly a yogī, identified with the supreme reality and he is a doer of all actions.[190] How can one see action in inaction? One can see that

---

187 … *loka-saṅgraham-evāpi sampaśyan-kartum-arhasi,* Bhagavadgītā, 3-20.

188 Ibid., 3-25.

189 *na buddhi-bhedaṁ janayed-ajñānāṁ karma-saṅginām,* Bhagavadgītā, 3-26.

190 *karmaṇy-akarma yaḥ paśyed-akarmaṇi ca karma yaḥ,* Bhagavadgītā, 4-18.

by realizing the fact that despite the absence of external activities, no one can be completely free from all internal mental activities. But, how can one see inaction in action? One can see this by realizing the fact that the real agency of all actions belongs to the guṇas of Prakṛti, and not to the immutable pure consciousness of the soul. That is, the guṇas are behind all the actions, while the soul remains inactive, merely witnessing all the activities. Thus, a person who can see action in inaction and inaction in action, understands the natures of both the soul as well as the world and its activities. Such a person is spiritually enlightened and hence identified with the Brahman. As such, he is a true yogī. Being identified with the Brahman, which is omnipresent and immanent in the world, he can also be treated as the doer of all activities. That is why the Bhagavadgītā says that a person who understands the natures of both action and inaction, is truly a spiritual master. He understands properly the nature of the soul, the nature of Prakṛti and its guṇas, as well as the immanence of Brahman in the world. In the case of such a spiritual master, all of his actions are devoid of resolutions, desires and objectives. His actions have gone through the heat treatment of spiritual knowledge and they have lost all their binding potency. Such spiritual adepts are referred to as *Puṇḍitas* even by the spiritual masters.[191]

Having become completely detached from all the results of performed actions, such a karma-yogī is ever content with his spiritual nature and does look to the world for anything. He remains grounded in and content with his spiritual realization. Even though he is seen performing various

---

[191] *jñānāgni-dagdha-karmāṇaṁ tamāhuḥ paṇḍitaṁ budhāḥ,* Bhagavadgītā, 4-19.

karmas, in reality, he does not perform any karma.[192] It is so because he is aware of his true identity as the pure and immutable soul, which is not at all involved with the functions of the physical body and the mind. He has complete control over internal organs, senses and the body. He is no longer engaged in amassing the things of worldly pleasures. Such a person performs only his basic duties and remains free from all demerits and karmic bondages.[193]

The perfected karma-yogī and *sthitaprajña* person remains content with the worldly gains that come of their own accord i.e. which are gained without making any focused and deliberate effort. He remains unaffected by the pairs of opposites e.g. pleasure and pain, heat and cold, joy and misery, health and disease, etc. He is completely free of jealousy. He remains even minded in the face of both success and failure. Such a karma-yogī does not get bound by karmic bondages, even though he is seen to be performing various karmas.[194] His attachment to the worldly entities has been completely eradicated. He is free from the illusory identification with the physical body and mind. His consciousness is ever established in the spiritual knowledge of the supreme Brahman. With such a state of consciousness, he remains ever engaged in the performance of *yajñas* only and as a result of this, technically speaking, all his karmas vanish i.e. they do not leave behind any subtle karmic consequences.[195] Here it should be borne in mind that *yajñas* basically refer to the actions of *loka-saṅgraha,* that is, the activities which are

---

[192] *...karmaṇy-abhiprvṛttopi naiva kiñcit-karoti saḥ,* Bhagavadgītā, 4-20.

[193] Ibid., 4-21.

[194] *...kṛtvāpi na nibadhyate,* Bhagavadgītā, 4-22.

[195] *... yajñāy- ācarataḥ karma samagraṁ pravilīyate,* Bhagavadgītā, 4-23.

designed to enhance the common good and welfare. The life and activities of the perfected karma-yogī, the *sthitaprajña,* themselves become akin to a Vedic *yajña,* a religious and ritual Vedic sacrifice. For such a sage, everything becomes identical with the supreme reality of Brahman. In the virtual Vedic sacrifice of his life and activities, the performer of the *yajña* is Brahman, the ladle is Brahman, the sacrificial fire is Brahman, the oblation is Brahman and the destination of the oblations too is Brahman. All his activities performed with such a state of mind, become virtually the supra-conscious state of *samādhi,* through which he attains to Brahman alone.[196] Apart from the *yajña* that is performed by the karma-yogī, aiming at *loka-saṅgraha,* there are numerous other kinds of *yajñas* described in the Vedic tradition, dealing with ritual and yogic practices. However, the *yajña* performed by the karma-yogī is of the form of niṣkāma-karmas, which are always aimed at *loka-saṅgraha* or the common good and welfare. The sage who has dedicated all his karmas through the performance of niṣkāma-karma, who has eradicated all his doubts through spiritual knowledge and who has perfect control over his mind and senses, never gets bound by the karmas or actions.[197] That is, such a person becomes free from karmic bondages and the cycle of rebirths.

Bhagavadgītā goes on to emphasize the point that Sāṅkhya and Yoga are not distinct from each other, as a person who practices any one of them effectively attains to the acclaimed result of both of them, namely Brahman.[198] Here Sāṅkhya refers to the path of spiritual knowledge or jñāna-yoga. In this path, the stress is on developing an intellectual

---

[196] *...brahmaiva tena gantavyaṁ brahma-karma-samādhinā,* Bhagavadgītā, 4-24.

[197] Ibid., 4-41.

[198] *sāṅkhya-yogau pṛthag-bālāḥ pravadanti na paṇḍitāḥ,* Bhagavadgītā, 5-4.

conviction about the spiritual nature of our self and its identity with the supreme immutable Brahman, which is immanent everywhere. As a result of such conviction, one transcends the illusion of identity with the physical body and as a result, one also frees oneself from the attachment to all worldly experiences. This immediately implies that such a person would never engage in any action for the sake of selfish experiences or the fruits of his actions. He would be performing only his duties and that too in a detached manner, which is nothing but the pure practice of karma-yoga. On the other hand, a true karma-yogī remains completely detached from the anticipated results of the performed actions. This means he remains indifferent to the possible pleasant or unpleasant experiences arising from those actions and instead, keeps himself focussed on the performance of his duties and obligations only. Such indifference to the varied phenomenal experiences virtually amounts to a denial of the phenomenal illusion of bodily identification, which is actually a practice of the path of knowledge. Thus, the practice of niṣkāma-karma practically involves the practice of the path of knowledge as well. Thus, Sāṅkhya and Yoga i.e. paths of knowledge and action are non-distinct as they overlap each other and also lead to the same result. The difference is only in terms of the points of emphases. In fact, this absence of rigid distinction applies even to the case of Bhakti-yoga or the path of devotion. In the practice of the path of devotion, the devotee surrenders himself to God and all his actions are dedicated to God, only for the sake of his pleasure. In doing this, the devotee does not care for his own individual pleasant or unpleasant experiences and dedicates all his actions to God, as a matter of supreme duty. This is nothing but the practice of karma-yoga. In practising such all-out dedication and surrender to God, the devotee thinks of his self as a spark or creation of God, thus denying his bodily identification at the phenomenal plane and he also tries to be convinced of the omnipresent immanence of God, which is nothing but the practice of the path of knowledge. Thus, all the three paths to spiritual realization and liberation enunciated in the Bhagavadgītā are interconnected and overlapping. Their difference lies only in terms of emphases. That is why the Bhagavadgītā declares that one who sees the identity of the path of knowledge and the path of action, rightly sees the whole matter.[199]

If at all there is some purpose behind the performance of niṣkāma-karma, then it cannot be anything other than the purification of the mind and internal organ, which is directly responsible for the highest spiritual realization and liberation.[200] That is, the karma-yogī has no material and phenomenal objective to achieve through the performance of his duties. The only objective that he strives for is spiritual upliftment and realization. However, even this spiritual objective is not a necessary component of karma-yoga, because karma-yoga can be perfectly practised even without having any spiritual objective whatsoever. But the fact remains that even when it is practised without the spiritual objective, its successful practice nonetheless ultimately culminates into the highest spiritual realization and liberation.

That person alone is a true renunciant, a true *saṁnyāsī*, and a true yogī or a karma-yogī, who does not get attached to the anticipated fruits of his actions and restricts his activities to only his duties and obligations.[201] The person who renounces

---

199 *ekaṁ sāṅkhyaṁ ca yogaṁ ca yaḥ paśyati sa paśyati,* Bhagavadgītā, 5-5.

200 *...yoginaḥ karma kurvanti saṅgaṁ tyaktvātmaśuddhaye,* Bhagavadgītā, 5-11.

201 *anāśritaḥ karma-phalaṁ kāryaṁ karma karoti yaḥ,*

his duties and other actions externally only, without becoming totally detached from its results and still has his mind fixed on various worldly activities and experiences, is neither a renunciant nor a yogī, but a hypocrite. True renunciation and true karma-yoga are one and the same.[202] Thus, true renunciation does not require one to move away from family and society. One may very well stay in his family and society, but he must carry on with his duties, with a sense of complete detachment to their results. Thus, Bhagavadgītā teaches a harmonious synthesis of the phenomenal welfare and spiritual evolution.

For a person who desires to attain the state of yoga, his practice of duties in a detached manner, is said to be the means of attaining that perfected state of yoga. But a person who has already perfected the art of niṣkāma-karma and is hence firmly rooted in yoga, there is a complete cessation of karmas and this cessation is said to be the cause or indicator of his firm rooting in yoga.[203] The perfected karma-yogī has a complete cessation of karmas in the special sense that because of his spiritual realization he is aware of his transcendent nature of the self and he finds only the guṇas being involved in all the activities. Whatever actions are performed by such a karma-yogī in the world, are naturally devoid of all attachments and even devoid of the sense of agency. Thus, what was an effortful practice of a spiritual discipline for the spiritual aspirant, becomes perfectly effortless and natural for the perfected spiritual master and this itself becomes the surest indicator of his spiritual realization and liberation. Thus, the spiritual

---

sa sannyāsī ca yogī ca na niragnirna cākriyaḥ, Bhagavadgītā, 6-1.

[202] *yaṁ sannyāsam-iti prāhur-yogaṁ taṁ viddhi pāṇḍava,* Bhagavadgītā, 6-2.

[203] Bhagavadgītā, 6-3.

master does not perform any activity in the normal sense of the term, yet externally, he seems to be vigorously engaged in actions. He does not have any personal identity and objective, with which he may engage in an action. He has become aware of his ontological identity with the omnipresent supreme Brahman, as well as the illusoriness of phenomenal identities and activities. His consciousness is firmly rooted in its identity with the absolute Brahman and whatever is done through his mortal frame, is but a reflection of the wish of that supreme consciousness, namely Brahman. A person is said to be firmly rooted in yoga or spiritual identity when his consciousness becomes completely devoid of all personal resolves and desires.[204] Such a spiritual master and perfected karma-yogī is called a *yogārūḍha* person.

Thus, Bhagavadgītā presents a multi-faceted discussion on the nature and desirability of karma-yoga. It shows the phenomenal and spiritual worthiness of niṣkāma-karma or detached actions. It has shown the various characteristics of a person following the path of karma-yoga. It has elaborately discussed the characteristics of a perfected karma-yogī. It has also discussed the overlapping nature of the three paths to liberation. Thus, the concepts of niṣkāma-karma and karma-yoga have been richly discussed in the Bhagavadgītā.

4.2 Significance of Niṣkāma-Karma for Spiritual Realization

Karma-yoga is one of the three paths to spiritual realization and liberation that have been discussed in the Bhagavadgītā. The path of karma-yoga involves the performance of detached actions or niṣkāma-karma. Niṣkāma-

[204] *sarva-saṅkalpa-sannyāsī yogārūḍhas-tadocyate,* Bhagavadgītā, 6-4.

karma basically means performing actions without having any attachment to the anticipated results of that action. But the moot point is why and how is performance of detached actions or niṣkāma-karma capable of leading to spiritual realization and liberation. In order to understand this potential of niṣkāma-karma, we first need to comprehend properly the nature of spiritual bondage, ignorance and illusion. We have already seen that from the highest viewpoint, reality is an immutable absolute, which has been variously referred to as Brahman, God and Ātman in the Bhagavadgītā. Being a transcendent absolute, it does not undergo any real ontological changes and it transcends space, time, causality, reason and language. However, this ontological fact does not provide an explanation of the world of space, time and plurality. It calls for a proper explanation.

This explanation comes from the concept of Brahma- śakti, the inalienable power of Brahman, which is also known as Māyā and Prakṛti. This Māyā, which is the inalienable power of Brahman, is instrumental in the epistemic obstruction of the self-awareness of the indivisible nature of Brahman. As a result of such, consciousness temporarily forgets its universal indivisible nature. Alongside this epistemic process, another epistemic process takes place and that is the epistemic projection of the world of space, time, causality, plurality, reason and language. One may try understand both these epistemic phenomena with the help of the dream analogy. Now, in a dream situation, it is only our consciousness that is at play. No external physical or material factor directly contributes in the making of the dream world. It is one's consciousness alone which makes itself epistemically appear as all the material and conscious entities of the dream world. Not only that, it also restricts its identity to a limited self in that dream world, which then seems to be witnessing and interacting with the dream world. While doing all this, the consciousness becomes totally oblivious of its own indivisible immanence through all the entities of the dream world. It totally seems to forget its ontological nature as the basic support of the entire dream world. It remains aware of itself only as a limited mortal human or non-human personality in the dream world, which goes through various kinds of experiences in the dream world, not knowing in the least that it is all but a dream and not reality. But, when one comes out of dream and wakes up, then one immediately and intuitively realises the illusory nature of the entire dream world and also comes to know that the dream world was nothing but a playful epistemic projection of his own consciousness, in which all the experiences of pleasure and pain, knowledge and ignorance, good and bad, etc. were equally illusory. Thus, the dream world appears real only as long as the dream continues. The termination of the dream immediately reveals its illusoriness as well as the ontologically unchanging nature of one's consciousness. One comes to understand intuitively that no real change in the consciousness had taken place even when the dream was manifesting itself. So, the ontologically immutable nature of one's consciousness may be seen to be consistent with the temporary epistemic obstruction of the self - awareness of consciousness, as well as with the epistemic projection of plurality, space, time, causality, reason, language, etc. in the dream world.

When this dream analogy is applied to the cosmic situation, one may speculate about the possibility of the entire cosmos being an illusory projection on and by the immutable universal consciousness, which has itself epistemically become everything and which is itself witnessing it and going through various kinds of experiences. In this scenario, the nature of spiritual bondage turns out to be just a case of epistemic illusion. Thus, spiritual bondage can be overcome through the eradication of epistemic illusion, which is possible only through proper spiritual knowledge. But mere theoretical knowledge would not suffice. One must be intuitively convinced of that spiritual knowledge and also act in accordance with that knowledge. The processes of spiritual knowledge and spiritual action mutually reinforce each other and together progress towards the culminating point of the complete eradication of spiritual ignorance and illusion, which then reveals the basic ontological identity of the self with Brahman. So, the spiritual discipline required for overcoming spiritual ignorance and illusion comprises of both intellectual and practical components.

Now, in the practice of niṣkāma-karma or detached karmas, one needs to be completely detached to the possible anticipated results of the performed action. This means, one needs to be completely indifferent to the various possible experiences that one may have to go through as a result of performing that action. But, remaining completely indifferent to the various possible experiences logically implies remaining indifferent to the various psycho-physical experiences undergone by our physical bodies. Thus, the practice of niṣkāma-karma effectively ensures that we deny the acknowledgement of the various experiences borne by our physical personalities. The continuous practice of such denial gradually weakens our belief about our basic identity with the physical body as well as our sense of being limited to the physical body. This weakening of the basic spiritual illusion is destined to ultimately culminate in the eradication of the illusory cosmic dream, which then immediately reveals the absolute nature of Brahman. So, the practice of niṣkāma-karma amounts to wilful denial of the dictates of spiritual illusion by trying to remain indifferent to our sense of bodily identification. Such continuous wilful denial helps in overcoming the basic spiritual illusion of bodily identification. It is the illusion of bodily identification which leads to the generation of all sorts of attachments and aversions in the light of our pleasant and unpleasant experiences. These attachments and aversions are the causes of our selfishly motivated worldly actions, which tie us in karmic bonds, leading to the cycle of transmigration. Therefore, refusing to be guided by the nature of bodily experiences and remaining completely detached to the results of performed karmas amounts to hitting directly at the basic form of spiritual illusion, namely bodily identification. Therefore, the practice of karma-yoga, i.e. the continuous practice of niṣkāma-karma, hits directly at the basic spiritual illusion and weakens it and ultimately eradicates it. Once the basic spiritual illusion gets eradicated, the pure nature of the self automatically manifests itself at the intuitive plane. This self-revelation does not require anything else at all. Just as coming out of the dream situation is by itself sufficient to reveal the true nature of both the dream and the consciousness, or just as the removal of covering over a light source is by itself sufficient to reveal the nature of that light source, similarly the mere eradication of the basic illusion of bodily identification is by itself sufficient to reveal the true nature of the self and consciousness, as being ontologically identical with the transcendent Brahman. This intuitive revelation immediately amounts to spiritual enlightenment and liberation from the cycle of transmigration. It is the state of a *sthitaprajña* or a perfected karma-yogi or a *yogāruḍha* Yogī. Thus, the continuous practice of niṣkāma-karma is by itself an effective spiritual discipline which has the capacity to take one to the pinnacle of spiritual knowledge and realization, without necessarily presuming anything about transcendental spiritual matters. Thus, even an atheist can attain spiritual realization through niṣkāma-karma.

4.3 Niṣkāma-Karma as Duty

The concept of duty is intimately connected with the sense of ought. The normative and injunctive stress in the concept of duty is its unique defining characteristic. To say that niṣkāma-karma or detached action is a duty, amounts to declaring that detached actions ought to be done. This naturally raises the question about the justification of attaching the ought sense with it. Why should one act in a detached manner?

In order to answer this question, we first need to appreciate that in ethics, there are broadly speaking, two ways of approaching this question. One is through the deontological route and the other one is through the consequentialist approach. Let us first take up the deontological approach. In this approach, it is a matter of duty that one ought to act in a certain manner. It is a matter of categorical imperative that has to be carried out, irrespective of all personal and circumstantial conditions. Bhagavadgītā is traditionally believed to present the gist of all the Upaniṣads, which in turn are believed to present the gist of the Vedas. The Vedic tradition believes that the Vedas are primarily injunctive and hence it is a categorical imperative for the followers of the Vedic tradition to adhere to the injunctions of the Vedas. Hence, the exhortation of the Bhagavadgītā regarding the practice of karma-yoga must be taken as a categorical ought. That is, the followers of the Vedic tradition must practice niṣkāma-karma as a matter of unconditional duty. Moreover, a large section of the Vedic community believes in the divinity of Lord Kṛṣṇa. This belief also requires one to treat the commands of Kṛṣṇa as a matter of unconditional duty. Therefore, for the followers of the Vedic tradition the teaching of Bhagavadgītā regarding niṣkāma-karma can be easily appreciated as a matter of unconditional duty.

But what would be the situation of people falling outside the Vedic fold? In order to understand this, we may take the help of Kant's criterion of duty in terms of universalizability and treating all human beings as an end, and never as a mere means. With reference to the universalizability criterion, we can easily see that attending to one's given duties in a completely detached manner will not lead to any inconsistency or internal conflicts. On the contrary, since various duties are designed and defined for the common welfare only, therefore, a detached performance of only duties by everyone would automatically lead to an ideal situation for the family, society, state and the world at large. Hence, with reference to the universalizability criterion, niṣkāma-karma can be clearly treated as a universal duty, carrying an unconditional ought with it. Now, as far as the other requirement of treating all human beings as an end, and never as a means, is concerned, it can be easily seen that if someone performs only his duties in a perfectly detached manner there would be no possibility of treating any human being as a mere means, because all duties aim at the common good and never at any selfish good. In fact, Bhagavadgītā goes even further than Kant and says that one should be treating not only the human beings, but all beings *per se* in an equally respectable manner, seeing the presence of God in all of them. Thus, it is clear that even for persons falling outside the purview of the

Vedic fold, it is possible to treat niṣkāma-karma as a categorical imperative or an unconditional duty.

Now, let us try to assess the possibility of treating niṣkāma-karma as a duty from the consequentialist viewpoint. Now, let us divide this assessment into two parts. The first part would look at the possible consequences for the self or the agent of detached actions. The second part would look at the consequences for the rest of the world. Now, in order to appreciate the likely consequences for the self, it would be fruitful to see that the usual actions undertaken by the worldly people are guided by selfish motivations, usually aiming at some kind of psycho-physical gratification or pleasure. The realization of such aims further grows attachment to them and leads to even more desires, which certainly cannot be realized beyond a point and thus eventually lead to disappointment, misery and frustration. On the other hand, if the desired goals are not realized in the beginning itself, then they immediately lead to disappointment, misery and frustration. Thus, in both the possible situations of success and failure, the motivational nature of worldly actions is such that they eventually lead to disappointment, misery and frustration. Obviously, this is not an ideal or desirable situation, even in worldly terms. Further, in spiritual terms, all such selfishly motivated actions inevitably lead to karmic bondage and keep one entangled in the cycle of transmigration. Thus, both phenomenally and spiritually, the usual worldly actions lead to undesirable consequences for the self.

Now, if a person performs his duties only and that too in a completely detached manner, then whatever may be the outcome of that action, he would not feel disappointed, miserable and frustrated about it. His mental poise would not be disturbed by any possible outcome of his action. On the other hand, the performance of one's duties in the spirit of niṣkāma-karma does not lead to any karmic bondage, according to Bhagavadgītā. Therefore, in both phenomenal and spiritual terms, the performance of one's duties in the spirit of niṣkāma-karma is highly beneficial and desirable for the self. Hence, from the consequentialist viewpoint, karma-yoga or performing one's duties in the spirit of niṣkāma-karma, can and definitely should be treated as a great duty for all.

Now, let us try to assess the possibility of treating niṣkāma-karma as a duty, from the consequentialist viewpoint, with reference to the world at large, and not just the self. We must first take note of the fact that any duty is never designed to serve the selfish ends of any given individual. All duties are usually designed to serve the common good, whether it is in the context of the family, society, state or the world at large. Therefore, the performance of one's various duties in spirit of detachment i.e. as niṣkāma-karma, by anyone will surely bring the enhancement of the common good. If everyone carries out his duty in the spirit of niṣkāma-karma, then the common good of world would be naturally maximized and that would be the realization of an ideal situation, in phenomenal terms.

In the light of the above discussion, it is clear that from both the phenomenal and spiritual viewpoints, as well as from the deontological and consequentialist considerations, that considering niṣkāma-karma as a duty and attaching the sense of ought with it, is not only clearly justified but also highly desirable. It is desirable for not only the followers of the Vedic tradition, but also for people falling outside that fold. Further, it should be treated as a highly desirable duty not only by people believing in God, but also by the atheists. That is, irrespective of all considerations, niṣkāma-karma is worthy of being treated as a supreme duty.

Chapter 5:
Spiritual Nature and Value of Wei-Wu-Wei

Historically speaking, Taoism has two distinct phases, where the earlier Taoism is associated with Lao-Tse and Chauang-Tzu. Amongst the various concepts discussed by early Taoism, the concept of Wei-Wu-Wei holds a central position and it is crucial to the entire framework of Taoism. It is important as a spiritual discipline, as well as the characteristic feature of the Tao realized sage. It has many aspects related to its discussion. These varied aspects of *wei-wu-wei* would become clear in the light of relevant passages from the Tao-Teh-Ching. *Wei-wu-wei* as duty would be the focus of this chapter, but before that it is vital to properly understand the concept of *wei-wu-wei* itself, in the light of Tao-Teh-Ching.

5.1 The Concept of Wei-wu-wei

The term *wei-wu-wei* is itself a puzzle to understand. Wei stands for action and wu stands for negation or denial (of something). Wu is also one of the names for the higher Tao. So, *wu-wei* would refer to the negation or denial of action. It may be simply put as non-action. When we prefix *wei* to *wu-wei* it represents the action that is characterized by non-action. So, *wei-wu-wei* may be simply translated as action in and through non-action. For the purpose of simplicity, we may translate it as action in non-action. So, the basic connotation of *wei-wu-wei* emerges as action that is characterized by non-action.

In order to understand the significance of *wei-wu-wei,* we need to bear in mind the primary meaning of Tao, which is the way. It refers to the way of reality, the way of nature, the way of heaven and the way of the Tao itself. Taoism primarily prescribes one to follow the path of the Tao, the path of nature and the path of reality. Taoism vehemently opposes all artificially created values and practices. It exhorts all to go back to the nature and live a life of natural simplicity. It even goes to the extent of criticizing the worldly quest for knowledge and power. Identification with the physical material body and the desire to fulfill the resultant aspirations, form the very crux of material life and Taoism opposes this very material life and its associated values. Now, the actions of the worldly people are guided by selfish motivations such as attachment, aversion, anger, greed, lust, jealousy, etc. All such emotions and aspirations are ultimately grounded in our sense of bodily identification and delimitation. All such worldly actions are termed *wei* or action in the normal sense of the term. Taoism talks of the negation or denial of all such worldly actions, that is, *wu-wei* in the sense of absence of worldly actions, which boils down to the requirement of the absence of all selfish motivations behind the actions. Thus, *wu-wei* represents the absence of all selfish worldly motivations and desires. It represents the complete riddance of the mind from all worldly motivations and desires. When the mind becomes empty of all worldly desires and aspirations, it is called the state of *hsu* or emptiness. Thus, *hsu* and *wu-wei* are two faces of the same coin. Both of them represent the absence of all worldly desires and aspirations. Now, when this state of freedom from all worldly desires becomes the characteristic mark of an action, then that is known as *wei-wu-wei.* So, *wei-wu-wei* or action in non-action stands for such actions which are characterized by the absence of all worldly desires. This naturally raises the question whether any action would be possible in that situation. In answer to this doubt, Taoism points out to the nature and says that it is the way of nature to act without any selfish motivations. The sun, the rain, the rivers, the plants and trees, all do their functions without any selfish motivations, benefitting the world at large. The covering of artificial worldly desires takes us away from nature and our own true forms. We move away from the path of nature and then our inherent peace and harmony gets disturbed, making us suffer all sorts of miseries and frustrations. Therefore, it is important and imperative to return back to the path of the Tao and the path of the nature, in order to restore the peace and harmony that is characteristic of the Tao.

Thus, *wei-wu-wei* represents actions that are characterized by the *hsu* or emptiness of all worldly desires and motivations. But, how can the *hsu* itself be realized? In order to realize *hsu,* one needs to practice solitude and silence. One has to willfully undo the artificial worldly values and customs. One has to continue with this effort until one's mind and heart become completely free of all worldly desires. Now, when this *hsu* or emptiness has been attained, the question arises what would that person do. When his mind has become empty of all selfish bodily motivations, then what would be the nature of his engaging in actions? The answer to this question lies in the Taoist concept of *fan* or the law of reversion. This law of reversion or *fan* basically states that there is a cosmic pattern in the motion of all changes. Each and everything start form its origin, going in its given direction up to the extreme end and then reverts back to merge in its origin. This mergence into the origin is the fulfillment of the destiny of that particular entity.

Everything in this phenomenal world follows the *fan.* It is the direct manifestation of the Tao in this world. In fact, the law of *fan* is illustrated by the Tao itself and since everything is rooted in the Tao, therefore *fan* is a basic and inalienable characteristic of this world. But, how does the Tao illustrate the *fan* itself? In the Taoist metaphysics, the ultimate ontological reality is the absolute and transcendent Tao. This higher transcendent Tao then manifests itself as the lower Tao or Teh, which is the same as God. The Teh then goes on to manifest and create the phenomenal world of plurality. In this phenomenal world everything follows the law of reversion and moves towards their in-built destinies. But after a while, the entire created world also merges back into Teh, and after that Teh itself merges back into the higher transcendent Tao. Thus, the cyclic nature of change is an inherent characteristic of the Tao itself. The world being the manifestation of the Tao, therefore, illustrates this cyclic nature of change as the most basic law of nature, followed by all phenomenal entities. Thus, everything follows its natural course of changes, which is designed to culminate in its mergence in its origin or the starting point. Since everything ultimately springs from the Tao itself, therefore the ultimate destiny of everything is merging back into the transcendent Tao. Thus, everything follows a natural course of events and changes that is inherently designed to take it to its ultimate destiny and origin. From this it follows that even if there is a complete absence of all worldly desires and aspirations, it would be wrong to think that there would be a complete cessation of actions. The natural and in-built current of changes, epitomizing the law of reversion or *fan,* would be sufficient to propel one to act in various ways in the world. Since all such actions would be illustrations of *wei-wu-wei,* they would be in perfect accord with the law of reversion or *fan*. As such, the practice of *wei-wu-wei* would necessarily take one closer to the realization of Tao as the universally immanent and transcendent reality, as well as the sole and absolute reality. The practice of *wei-wu-wei* requires emptiness or *hsu* as its prerequisite. Obviously, *hsu* cannot be achieved all of sudden. It has to be gradually cultured through the practice of solitude, silence and staying away from the worldly environment, values and practices. One has to gradually get rid of all the artificial worldly coverings cast over the self, in order to move closer to the Tao and ultimately realize it as the absolute transcendent reality. With the perfection of *wei-wu-wei*, one comes to realize intuitively the nature of the self and the nature of everything as Tao. One becomes a *ming*, an enlightened one. With this enlightenment comes the complete riddance from all worldly desires and aspirations and then *hsu* or emptiness becomes perfect. When *hsu* gets perfected, the practice of *wei-wu-wei* too becomes perfect. Such perfection of *wei-wu-wei* becomes the characteristic of a *ming* or a Tao realized person. The actions of such a realized person are in perfect harmony with nature and completely free from all worldly desires and aspirations. The illustrative actions of a perfect *wei-wu-wei* are prompted by the universal law of reversion or *fan*. Therefore, the actions illustrative of a perfect *wei-wu-wei* have their roots in the sage's intuitive realization of the Tao as the universal and absolute transcendent ontological reality. In this way, the practice of *wei-wu-wei* can be broadly classified into two categories. The first kind of *wei-wu-wei* represents the deliberate and effortful practice of *wei-wu-wei* and *hsu*, which is necessarily far from perfect and is basically the practice of the Taoist spiritual discipline. Continuous refinement of this discipline ultimately leads to the intuitive realization of the Tao. Such realization immediately brings about the perfection of the *hsu* and the *wei-wu-wei.* This is the second category of *wei-wu-wei,* where it becomes absolutely effortless and natural for the Tao realized person. Thus, a perfect *wei-wu-wei* is the characteristic hallmark of the realization of Tao. It is the outer sign of a perfect spiritual realization.

Now, let us take a look at some of the illustrative passages of the Tao-Teh-Ching which shed light on the various aspects of *wei-wu-wei.* Tao-Teh-Ching points out in the beginning itself that being free from all worldly desires is a prerequisite for the proper grasping of the nature of Tao.[205] Such complete freedom from the worldly desires is called *hsu.* Without it, one can only touch the fringes of the nature of Tao. It is so because the covering of worldly desires over our minds takes us away from our true nature as the Tao. The true nature of our selves is no longer visible to us. Hence, *hsu* is imperative for the proper understanding of the Tao. Then, Tao-Teh-Ching goes on to point out the necessary complementarity of the two extreme polarities of any conception and entity. It starts with the necessary complementarity of existence and non-existence, which respectively refer to the lower and the higher Tao, or Teh and Tao.[206] It says that existence and non-existence give birth to each other. That is, they are each other's origin and culmination. Conceptually also, they always arise simultaneously. The idea of one brings along the idea of the other as well. Similarly, in the phenomenal sphere, all sorts of entities and conceptions take shape in the form of dual polarities and it is witnessed in the world that continuous

---

[205] Legge, James, Tr. *Tao-Teh-Ching,* 1-3, www.FreeSpiritualEbooks.com, 2008.

[206] Legge, James, Tr. *Tao-Teh-Ching,* 2-2, www.FreeSpiritualEbooks.com, 2008.

change keeps taking place between the two extremes. Such continuous change taking place from one extreme to the other and vice-versa is called *fan* or the law of reversion. This law is followed by each and every entity in the world and it represents the most fundamental law of nature. This fundamental law itself derives from the nature of the dual polarity of the Tao and Teh. Thus, one may think of *fan* or the law of reversion as the direct manifestation of the nature of Tao at the phenomenal plane. This law shows the necessity of continuous change and the cyclic nature of these changes in the world with respect to all its entities. Therefore, due to the inviolable nature of changes taking place in the format of dual polarities, the enlightened sage goes beyond these dualistic changes by totally ridding his mind from all phenomenal desires and aspirations. This complete riddance ensures his cessation from all worldly activities or selfish motivated actions, which means, all of his actions become the illustrations of *wei-wu-wei*. Such a practice of the perfected *wei-wu-wei* is the external characteristic of the Tao realized sage.

Wei-wu-wei is illustrated in the natural processes of growth and accomplishment, as well as in the working of the lower Tao, the creator of the entire world. All the tasks are completed, but there is no claim of ownership or accomplishment in the case of all natural processes and the activities of the lower Tao i.e. Teh.[207] This complete absence of ego and ownership is the sign of the perfect *wei-wu-wei*. So, *wei-wu-wei* is perfectly exhibited in the works of nature, in the actions of the Tao realized sage, as well as in the case of Tao itself. The Tao realized sage tries to keep the people away from

---

[207] Legge, James, Tr. *Tao-Teh-Ching*, 2-4, www.FreeSpiritualEbooks.com, 2008.

worldly knowledge and desires, since only then the practice of *wei-wu-wei* would become possible and there would be the possibility of moving closer to the realization of the Tao.[208] Tao-Teh-Ching compares the nature of the Tao with the emptiness of a vessel, thereby trying to show the complete absence of all phenomena and phenomenal desires in the Tao.[209] Such perfect emptiness or *hsu* of the mind of the realized sage is the characteristic feature of his realization. His mind is completely free from all phenomenal desires and aspirations, just as the Tao is free from all phenomena. Such perfect *hsu* is the necessary precondition for the practice of the perfect *wei-wu-wei* or action in non-action. This *hsu* has to be gradually cultivated through the practice of solitude, silence and withdrawal from the worldly environment.

Throwing light on the nature and behavior of the Tao realized sages, Tao-Teh-Ching points out that they do not have any inner motivation of deliberately being benevolent to one and all. Rather, they treat all in an equal manner and their benevolence to all flows out of their Tao realization, as a matter of necessity and not out of choice.[210] The natural benevolence of the Tao realized sage flows from his realization and is the characteristic feature of his *wei-wu-wei* or action in non-action. Thus, the perfection of *wei-wu-wei* is the natural outcome of the realization of Tao. Referring to the enduring nature of heaven and earth, Tao-Teh-Ching points out their unselfish nature and

---

[208] Legge, James, Tr. *Tao-Teh-Ching,* 3-3, www.FreeSpiritualEbooks.com, 2008.

[209] Legge, James, Tr. *Tao-Teh-Ching,* 4-1, www.FreeSpiritualEbooks.com, 2008.

[210] Legge, James, Tr. *Tao-Teh-Ching,* 5-1, www.FreeSpiritualEbooks.com, 2008.

presents it as the cause of their endurance.[211] This also seeks to present the way of nature as comprising of unselfishness. Thus, to follow the Tao or way of nature means to practice unselfishness. Therefore, the Tao realized sage never thinks of his own place or importance, being totally bereft of all ego and pride; yet, the Tao ensures that all his personal needs are fulfilled.[212] Tao-Teh-Ching beautifully points out the irony that it is because of the sage's relegation of his ego and pride that the Tao itself takes full care of his personal needs. Thus, when a person empties his mind and heart of all selfish desires and worldly motivations, his practice of *hsu* becomes perfect, and when the *hsu* is perfected, the practice of *wei-wu-wei* also becomes perfect, which then immediately opens up the gates of Tao realization. Thus, *wei-wu-wei* requires *hsu* as its precondition, while it is itself the immediate cause and characteristic feature of Tao realization. Talking of the highest excellence, Tao-Teh-Ching compares it with water and its characteristic features.[213] Water is beneficial to everyone and it naturally occupies the lowest position available to it. Similarly, the sage is inherently beneficial to every being and he takes the lowliest position, without any complaints, because he is totally free from all ego and pride. This universal benevolence and lack of ego is the way of Tao; hence, the sage is nearer to the Tao and he illustrates the nature of the Tao in his character. The actions of the sage are without any ego and selfishness and they thus exemplify emptiness of all worldly desires or *hsu*.

---

[211] Legge, James, Tr. *Tao-Teh-Ching*, 7-1, www.FreeSpiritualEbooks.com, 2008.

[212] Legge, James, Tr. *Tao-Teh-Ching*, 7-2, www.FreeSpiritualEbooks.com, 2008.

[213] Legge, James, Tr. *Tao-Teh-Ching*, 8-1, www.FreeSpiritualEbooks.com, 2008.

The characteristic of the perfect *hsu* ensures, in turn, that all the actions of the sage turn out to be illustrations of *wei-wu-wei.*

Talking of wealth and worldly honours, Tao-Teh-Ching points out that when they get associated with a person, then they surely generate ego and pride also in the mind of that person. Thus, worldly excellence begets its own evil, which takes one away from the way of the Tao.[214] Therefore, the Tao realized sage retires into oblivion, when his natural benevolent actions start generating worldly praise and honour. Silent benevolence and later withdrawal into oblivion is the way of the Tao and this is illustrated by the Tao realized sage. The Tao is the source of everything. It produces all and also sustains everything, but it never shows off itself as the creator, sustainer and controller of all entities; it is free of all ego and pride.[215] Tao-Teh-Ching calls this the mysterious quality of the Tao. This mysterious quality also gets illustrated in the actions of the Tao realized sage. He exemplifies perfect *hsu,* and thus, all his actions are free from ego and selfish motivations. They all become examples of the perfect *wei-wu-wei* or action in non-action. They are all universally benevolent and devoid of ego and pride, just as the activities of the Tao are universally benevolent and devoid of ego and pride.

Tao-Teh-Ching beautifully brings out the difference between needs and desires by saying that former pertain to the belly, while the latter pertain to the eyes.[216] The natural

---

214 Legge, James, Tr. *Tao-Teh-Ching,* 9-2, www.FreeSpiritualEbooks.com, 2008.

215 Legge, James, Tr. *Tao-Teh-Ching,* 10-3, www.FreeSpiritualEbooks.com, 2008.

216 Legge, James, Tr. *Tao-Teh-Ching,*12-2, www.FreeSpiritualEbooks.com, 2008.

requirements of the physical body are one's needs, to which the sage caters. He fulfils only the natural needs for survival and does not strive to attain the things and experiences which do not belong to one's natural constitution, but have been picked up from the external world through the senses. Thus, the non-egoistic non-selfish actions of the sage are designed to cater to only the basic needs of nature and not for attaining any selfish goals. His *wei-wu-wei* is designed for universal benevolence, having no traces of selfishness and worldly desires. Talking of the 'form of the formless' Tao, Tao-Teh-Ching refers to its ceaseless activities and how despite all that, it cannot even be named and how it ultimately merges back into nothingness.[217] Thus, despite all activities, Tao illustrates oblivion and relegation into nothingness. This nature of the Tao is illustrated in the *wei-wu-wei* of the Tao realized sage. The significance of *wei-wu-wei* is indicated by Tao-Teh-Ching by pointing out that although the Tao is beyond the reach of space, time, causality, reason and language, yet a clue to its universal and transcendent nature may be grasped if one follows the nature of Tao in his phenomenal actions.[218] Now, since the nature of the Tao is ceaseless activity, without a trace of ego, pride and selfishness, therefore, the practice of such activities in the world becomes the stepping stone to the realization of the Tao. Such activities are the examples of *wei-wu-wei,* hence, the practice of *wei-wu-wei* is required as an important spiritual discipline for getting closer to the Tao and ultimately realizing it. Thus, even though Tao-Teh-Ching highlights the inherent transcendence of the Tao, yet it also

---

[217] Legge, James, Tr. *Tao-Teh-Ching,*14-2, www.FreeSpiritualEbooks.com, 2008.

[218] Legge, James, Tr. *Tao-Teh-Ching,* 14-3, www.FreeSpiritualEbooks.com, 2008.

concedes the significant fact that through the practice of *wei-wu-wei* one moves closer to the realization of Tao and one may finally have the complete intuitive realization of the Tao. The knower of the mysterious Tao is also similarly mysterious to the worldly people.[219] In order to broadly identify the Tao realized master, Tao-Teh-Ching says that such a person is unpretentious, somewhat shrinking from the worldly people and environment, grave and also apparently dull and empty minded.[220] Thus, the Tao realized master does not exhibit any external eye-catching excellences. However, one characteristic is certainly visible to those having the eye for it. Such masters so not have any ego and pride. In this sense, they are empty of selfishness and worldliness.[221] They epitomize the perfection of *hsu*. This emptiness of worldly desires and selfishness ensures that their actions are only the ones that are prompted by their inner realization of the Tao. All such actions are the illustrations of the perfect *wei-wu-wei*. That is to say, the Tao realized masters naturally exhibit the perfection of *wei-wu-wei,* which is universally benevolent and devoid of all ego and worldly desires.

Pointing out the importance of *hsu,* Tao-Teh-Ching says that the emptiness of all worldly desires, selfishness and ego should be cultivated to the highest degree and the stillness of one's being, i.e. the consciousness of the mind, too should

---

[219] Legge, James, Tr. *Tao-Teh-Ching,* 15-1, www.FreeSpiritualEbooks.com, 2008.

[220] Legge, James, Tr. *Tao-Teh-Ching,* 15-2, www.FreeSpiritualEbooks.com, 2008.

[221] Legge, James, Tr. *Tao-Teh-Ching,* 15-4, www.FreeSpiritualEbooks.com, 2008.

reach perfection.[222] According to the law of reversion or *fan,* everything must ultimately reach its origin and become completely still. This stillness in its origin is the fulfillment of its destiny. Thus, the perfection of *hsu* and the stillness of one's mind and consciousness, mark the fulfillment of one's destiny, which means one has attained to one's origin, namely the higher Tao. This way, Tao-Teh-Ching has indicated the conditions required for attaining the realization of the Tao. Since *hsu* and *wei-wu-wei* are two faces of the same coin, therefore, the practice and perfection of *hsu, wei-wu-wei* and the stillness of one's mind and consciousness, jointly spell the spiritual disciplines required for the realization of the Tao. Further, one who understands the necessary law of reversion and the nature of the fulfillment of one's destiny, is said to be spiritually wise and close to the Tao. Such a master develops affinity with the whole world, as well as great capacity and forbearance.[223] He is said to be possessed of the Tao. Being thus one with the Tao, he becomes free from the fear of all decay and corruption.

Describing the state of a Tao realized master, Tao-Teh-Ching says that he is very different form the masses of worldly people. While the masses seem happy and intelligent, dealing with various affairs of the world, the Tao realized master seems dull and forlorn, not having any worldly desire whatsoever.[224] But, although he may seem isolated from all, he values the Tao and remains content with its inner realization

---

222 Legge, James, Tr. *Tao-Teh-Ching,* 16-1, www.FreeSpiritualEbooks.com, 2008.

223 Legge, James, Tr. *Tao-Teh-Ching,* 16-2, www.FreeSpiritualEbooks.com, 2008.

224 Legge, James, Tr. *Tao-Teh-Ching,* 20-2, www.FreeSpiritualEbooks.com, 2008.

and is continuously guided by that realization in the form of *wei-wu-wei* or action in non-action. Then, Tao-Teh-Ching also points out greatness of *hsu* and *wei-wu-wei.* Although the Tao realized sage is empty of all desires and ego, yet all his needs are fulfilled and his greatness is acknowledged by all. Although he relegates himself to the backdrop, yet he shines among all. Although he does not strive to attain anything, yet his attainments are incomparable in the world.[225] Those who pursue the course of the Tao, desist from having any ego and worldly desires and strive for extreme humility.[226] This effort leads to the perfection of emptiness or *hsu,* which then leads to the perfection of *wei-wu-wei.* Such a master does not leave behind any human being and the actions of his *wei-wu-wei* are beneficial for one and all.[227] He develops a sense of unity with all the entities in the world. This sense of unity engenders universal love and concern. Such a Tao realized master does not make deliberate efforts to achieve anything. He does not indulge in any activity for the sake of attaining anything.[228] All his activities are the illustrations of *wei-wu-wei,* which flow naturally and effortlessly out of his inner Tao realization. Through his *wei-wu-wei,* the sage is able to accomplish great things, but the root of such success lies in his not having any grand designs and objectives.[229] It is the utmost humility of the

---

[225] Legge, James, Tr. *Tao-Teh-Ching,* 22-2, www.FreeSpiritualEbooks.com, 2008.

[226] Legge, James, Tr. *Tao-Teh-Ching,* 24, www.FreeSpiritualEbooks.com, 2008.

[227] Legge, James, Tr. *Tao-Teh-Ching,* 27-1, www.FreeSpiritualEbooks.com, 2008.

[228] Legge, James, Tr. *Tao-Teh-Ching,* 29-2, www.FreeSpiritualEbooks.com, 2008.

[229] Legge, James, Tr. *Tao-Teh-Ching,* 34-3, www.FreeSpiritualEbooks.com, 2008.

sage that ensures the greatness of his accomplishments. Thus, the *hsu* that accompanies the *wei-wu-wei* of the sage, guarantees the grand success of the *wei-wu-wei*. The Tao, in its natural order, does nothing for the sake of doing it; hence, there is nothing that it does not do.[230] Similarly, when the Tao realized master practices *wei-wu-wei* due to his *hsu,* there is nothing that he aims for, yet there is nothing that he does not accomplish. Such a master, in his simplicity, humility, stillness and emptiness, does not deliberate on doing or achieving anything, yet everything goes exactly aright in his natural spiritual flow.[231]

Tao-Teh-Ching points out the uniqueness of Tao by saying that even though it is non-existence, yet everything is produced out of it and there is no place that is devoid of the Tao.[232] Similarly, even though *wei-wu-wei* is devoid of all motivations and objectives, yet there is nothing that it cannot achieve. It never fails in giving its due result. Water is the softest thing in the world, yet it is so effective in smoothening out the rough edges of the hard stones by continuously dashing against it. Thus, the strength and advantage of working in the spirit of *hsu* and *wei-wu-wei* are enormous, although very few people understand it. The rarity of the situation is indicated by Tao-Teh-Ching when it says that there are few people in the world who are able to attain the teaching and knowledge that is beyond the words, namely the realization of Tao, and also very few people who know and

---

230 Legge, James, Tr. *Tao-Teh-Ching,* 37-1, www.FreeSpiritualEbooks.com, 2008.

231 Legge, James, Tr. *Tao-Teh-Ching,* 37-3, www.FreeSpiritualEbooks.com, 2008.

232 Legge, James, Tr. *Tao-Teh-Ching,* 43-1, www.FreeSpiritualEbooks.com, 2008.

appreciate the value of *wei-wu-wei* or action in non-action.[233] Both Tao and *wei-wu- wei* are extremely subtle, yet highly impactful and pervasive in their effects. Further, the spiritual value and effectiveness of the purity and stillness of the mind is emphasized by Tao-Teh-Ching.[234] Here the purity of the mind refers to *hsu* or the emptiness of the mind of all worldly desires and ego, whereas stillness refers to the placidity of the consciousness in the face of all possible situations and experiences. The value of such purity and stillness lies in their potential to reveal the way of the Tao. That is to say, the practice and perfection of such purity and stillness reveals intuitively the right and spiritual way of living in the world, as also the very nature of the Tao itself. Thus, *hsu* and stillness of mind are the highest spiritual disciplines and virtues in Taoism, and *wei-wu-wei* follows them as their natural implication. In fact, *wei-wu-wei* may be understood as the external manifestation of such inner perfection and realization. Moreover, when the way of Tao, through the external manifestation and practice of *wei-wu-wei*, prevails in the world, there is all round peace and harmony, but when it is relegated, strife and misery encompass the world.[235] Thus, it becomes clear that following the way of Tao is vital not only for the esoteric spiritual value, but it is equally vital also for the phenomenal value of peace and harmony in the world at all levels. Tao-Teh-Ching indicates the nature, methodology and value of spiritual knowledge by pointing out that the farther

---

[233] Legge, James, Tr. *Tao-Teh-Ching*, 43-2, www.FreeSpiritualEbooks.com, 2008.

[234] Legge, James, Tr. *Tao-Teh-Ching*, 45-2, www.FreeSpiritualEbooks.com, 2008.

[235] Legge, James, Tr. *Tao-Teh-Ching*, 46-1, www.FreeSpiritualEbooks.com, 2008.

away one is from his self, the less he knows; and the closer one is to his self, the greater is his knowledge.[236] The self is ontologically one with the Tao. Therefore, the closer one is to the self, the closer one is to the Tao. This proximity to the Tao intuitively reveals the true nature of the Tao and the self. Since the Tao has become everything, therefore, understanding the true nature of Tao grants an intuitive insight into the nature of everything in the world. Yet, such pervasive knowledge is all intuitive; it does not require wandering in the world. Therefore, the Tao realized sage comes to know everything without making any effort to know. Similarly, through the perfection of *wei-wu-wei,* he accomplishes everything without making any deliberate effort to accomplish them.[237]

Contrasting the natures of worldly knowledge and spiritual knowledge, Tao-Teh-Ching says that the seeker of worldly knowledge goes on adding to his knowledge in an effortful manner, whereas the seeker of the knowledge of Tao goes on reducing his purposeful activities and acquired worldly knowledge.[238] Thus, seeking Tao is a matter of daily diminution, whereas seeking worldly knowledge is a matter of daily accretion. The seeker of the Tao goes on diminishing his worldly desires and purposeful activities till he arrives at the point of having no worldly desires whatsoever and he completely stops performing all purposeful activities.[239] This

---

[236] Legge, James, Tr. *Tao-Teh-Ching,* 47-1, www.FreeSpiritualEbooks.com, 2008.

[237] Legge, James, Tr. *Tao-Teh-Ching,*47-2, www.FreeSpiritualEbooks.com, 2008.

[238] Legge, James, Tr. *Tao-Teh-Ching,* 48-1, www.FreeSpiritualEbooks.com, 2008.

[239] Legge, James, Tr. *Tao-Teh-Ching,* 48-2, www.FreeSpiritualEbooks.com, 2008.

state depicts the perfection of *hsu* as well as *wei-wu-wei.* Having attained such spiritual perfection, the Tao realized master actually does everything, even without doing anything. That is to say, due to the intuitive realization of his ontological identity with the highest Tao, he is actually involved with all the activities of the universe, even when externally he is doing nothing. On the other hand, even when he seems to be vigorously engaged in various activities, he does not actually do anything because of his being free from all selfish motivations and worldly desires. Elaborating further the nature of *wei-wu-wei,* Tao-Teh-Ching says that when a person does not have any purpose or objective to realize and acts only according to his inner nature i.e. when a person illustrates the perfection of *wei-wu-wei,* he happens to attain everything in this world.[240] On the contrary, when a person seeks to attain various objectives in a deliberate and effortful manner, he cannot always be successful and thus he is sure to face misery and frustration.

Tao-Teh-Ching gives a very important clue about way the one should live in order to have a trouble-free life. It says, the Tao from which everything originates is the Mother of all things and beings. Each and every entity is but a child of that great Mother. Now, if one knows the nature of the mother of a child and tries to nourish and cultivate the characteristics of the mother in the child, then that child shall have a trouble-free life.[241] This indicates the suggestion that by knowing and cultivating the characteristics of the Tao in our daily lives and activities, we can live peaceful and harmonious lives. Thus, the

---

240 Legge, James, Tr. *Tao-Teh-Ching,* 48-3, www.FreeSpiritualEbooks.com, 2008.

241 Legge, James, Tr. *Tao-Teh-Ching,* 52-1,2, www.FreeSpiritualEbooks.com, 2008.

nature of the Tao gives us the *'ought'* according to which we should lead our lives. Thus, in Taoism, for the betterment of the self and the world at large, it becomes our duty to follow the nature of the Tao. The person who follows the nature of the Tao and practices the spiritual disciplines of *hsu, wei-wu-wei* and the stillness of the mind, ultimately realizes the nature of Tao and its identity with the self, as well as its identity with everything in the world, and as a result of that realization, he has nothing to fear throughout his phenomenal life.[242] The way of the Tao is really very simple and straight forward, but the worldly people choose the complicated alternative paths, and that too for the wrong ends.[243] Thus, instead of following the path of the simple *wei-wu-wei,* the worldly people go for the complicated ways to attain the worldly material goods and experiences. With reference to the Tao realized master, Tao-Teh-Ching says that he is like an infant; simple, lacking all ego, instinctive and energetic, having no fear from anything in the world.[244] Due to his attunement with the universally immanent Tao, he has nothing to fear in the world. The nature of the transcendent Tao is unfathomable and beyond all speech. Therefore, the Tao realized master has nothing to talk about it, but those who do not know it, are ever ready and boastful about the nature and description of the Tao.[245] Tao can only be realized intuitively and it is beyond the reach of logic and language. The Tao realized sage is beyond the

[242] Legge, James, Tr. *Tao-Teh-Ching,* 52-3, www.FreeSpiritualEbooks.com, 2008.

[243] Legge, James, Tr. *Tao-Teh-Ching,* 53-2, www.FreeSpiritualEbooks.com, 2008.

[244] Legge, James, Tr. *Tao-Teh-Ching,* 55-1, www.FreeSpiritualEbooks.com, 2008.

[245] Legge, James, Tr. *Tao-Teh-Ching,* 56-1, www.FreeSpiritualEbooks.com, 2008.

considerations of profit and loss, pleasure and pain, merit and demerit, as his practice of *hsu* and *wei-wu-wei* keep him utterly indifferent to the possible results of his activities.[246] Such a master engages in all activities in the natural flow of the Tao, without even being acutely aware of his effort and deliberation going into that action.[247] He does not feel the trouble involved in any activity due to his activities being the perfect illustrations of *wei-wu-wei.* Whatever he engages in, is the outcome of his inner spiritual prompting and his harmony with the Tao. Through all his activities, the Tao realized sage moves towards the natural development and harmony of all things, whereas the worldly people adopt all sorts of unnatural means for attaining their material goals. The sage not desire what the worldly people desire; he does not learn what the worldly people learn.[248] His actions are the illustrations of *wei-wu-wei,* springing from his inner spiritual nature, whereas the actions of the worldly people spring from their selfish material desires. Tao-Teh-Ching talks of three precious things which have great spiritual value, namely gentleness, economy and shrinking from taking precedence over others.[249] Gentleness is the way of Tao, for it never exerts itself in doing anything; everything happens in its natural flow. Economy shows the futility and inferiority of artificial worldly things. Shrinking from taking precedence over others shows the greatest spiritual value, namely humility. The Tao realized sage not

---

[246] Legge, James, Tr. *Tao-Teh-Ching,* 56-3, www.FreeSpiritualEbooks.com, 2008.

[247] Legge, James, Tr. *Tao-Teh-Ching,* 63-1, www.FreeSpiritualEbooks.com, 2008.

[248] Legge, James, Tr. *Tao-Teh-Ching,* 64-4, www.FreeSpiritualEbooks.com, 2008.

[249] Legge, James, Tr. *Tao-Teh-Ching,* 67-2, www.FreeSpiritualEbooks.com, 2008.

only acts due to his inner spiritual promptings, but he also does not cling to and claim as his own the results of his actions.[250] He does not stick to it. He never has any arrogance for his achievements. The realization of the Tao requires simplicity of the heart and mind. Therefore, the sages are seldom extensively learned, and extensively learned seldom come to realize the nature of Tao.[251] Through his *wei-wu-wei,* the sage does not seek to acquire anything for himself; yet, the more he gives to others, the more he acquires himself, i.e. the closer he comes to his self or the Tao.[252] The sage never strives for anything through his actions; hence, his actions are virtually non-actions i.e. *wei-wu-wei.*[253] Thus, the presuppositions, characteristics and implications of *wei-wu-wei* have been elaborately discussed in the Tao-Teh-Ching.

5.2 Significance of Wei-wu-wei for Spiritual Realization

In the context of Taoism, spiritual realization basically means returning to the Tao, living in accordance with the Tao and becoming free from all artificial values and desires. There is nothing to be acquired in spiritual realization, as the Tao is eternally everywhere in the world and it is also transcendent ontologically. Therefore, the realization of Tao requires one to be completely free from all worldly desires and values. But this

---

250 Legge, James, Tr. *Tao-Teh-Ching,* 77-4, www.FreeSpiritualEbooks.com, 2008.

251 Legge, James, Tr. *Tao-Teh-Ching,* 81-1, www.FreeSpiritualEbooks.com, 2008.

252 Legge, James, Tr. *Tao-Teh-Ching,* 81-2, www.FreeSpiritualEbooks.com, 2008.

253 Legge, James, Tr. *Tao-Teh-Ching,* 81-3, www.FreeSpiritualEbooks.com, 2008.

cannot happen in a moment. Then, what is to be done? In order to be completely free from all worldly desires and values, one must stop performing all activities aiming at worldly goals. Of course, this too cannot be done instantly. It requires a strong will and prolonged practice. Of course, one would move towards its perfection only in a gradual manner. But even while practicing it, what would be the nature of a spiritual aspirant's activities? If he is not aiming for worldly goals or acting out of selfish reasons, then what sort of activities would he engage in? The answer is to be found in *fan* or the law of reversion and the Taoist conception of the fulfillment of one's destiny. The law of reversion or *fan* basically holds that everything is constantly going through changes and direction of these changes is cyclic in nature. That is, starting from its origin, a given entity reaches its extreme point of growth and development, after which it starts changing in the direction of its originating point. Ultimately, it reaches and merges back in its point of origin. Such culmination in its point of origin is called the fulfillment of its destiny, attaining which it rests in absolute peace. Everything in the world follows this universal and fundamental law of nature. The universality of this law is a manifestation of the nature and epistemic manifestive process of the Tao. The transcendent higher Tao epistemically manifests itself as the lower Tao, which then goes on to create the world of phenomena. All of these phenomenal entities follow the law of reversion. Later on, the entire phenomenal world merges back into the lower Tao, which then further merges back into the higher transcendent Tao. This cyclic manifestation and merger of the Tao is the reason for the universality of the law of reversion, as everything in the world is ultimately rooted in the Tao alone. Thus, the law of reversion shows that all entities are necessarily going through changes and all of these changes are naturally directed towards their origins. This means there is a natural definite direction involved in all such changes. Therefore, even if there is no selfish motivation or artificial goal behind an action, some action or the other would definitely keep on taking place and there would be a natural direction involved in those actions. Thus, even when a person has attained the perfection of *hsu* i.e. complete emptiness of all selfish motivations and worldly desires, still he would be performing actions in accordance with the natural flow of the law of reversion or *fan*. Such actions are very different from the actions of the worldly people, as they do not spring from selfish motivations or anticipated material goals. In this sense, they may be called non-actions. Yet, they are actions nonetheless. Therefore, they are called action in non-action or *wei-wu-wei*.

Now, performing such *wei-wu-wei*, even imperfectly and in a deliberate manner, tends to empty the mind of worldly desires and values. Such continuous practice of performing *wei-wu-wei* gradually purges the mind of all worldliness, which is then instrumental in the intuitive realization of the Tao as the universal and transcendent ontological absolute, that is also the most basic nature of the self. Thus, there are two classes of *wei-wu-wei*. The first one refers to the *wei-wu-wei* that is practiced by the spiritual aspirant, in a somewhat imperfect and deliberate manner. It is accompanied by a similarly imperfect *hsu* or emptiness. Its continuous practice gradually takes the aspirant to the point of realization of Tao, by completely ridding the mind of all worldly desires and aspirations. Then, that person no longer remains a spiritual aspirant, but he becomes a Tao realized master. Such a person's mind is completely rid of all worldliness. Hence, ha has perfect *hsu* or emptiness of the mind. Due to such perfection of *hsu,* all of his actions spring from the nature of his inner spiritual promptings alone. Hence, all such actions become the perfect illustrations of *wei-wu-wei* or action in non-action. This is the second class of *wei-wu-wei.*

The practice of *wei-wu-wei* does not require one to have any theistic faith or belief in some transcendent ontological reality. The mere practice of ridding one's mind of artificial values and worldly desires is capable of cleansing one's mind and ultimately enable it to have the intuitive realization of the Tao. Thus, *wei-wu-wei* is highly effective, yet simple as a means of spiritual realization. Moreover, the perfect *wei-wu-wei* also becomes an external characteristic of the Tao realized master. Of course, *hsu* or emptiness is the prerequisite of *wei-wu-wei* and its perfection or imperfection directly determines the perfection or imperfection of the *wei-wu-wei.* This *hsu* or emptiness itself is to be cultivated through the practice of silence, solitude and withdrawal from the world. Thus, it can be said that *wei-wu-wei* constitutes the most important external spiritual discipline of Taoism, whereas *hsu* constitutes the most important mental discipline of Taoism, and both of them are intimately related with each other. They mutually reinforce each other and together evolve towards their perfection and the consequent realization of Tao. Thus, *wei-wu-wei* is a central discipline for spiritual realization in Taoism.

5.3 Wei-wu-wei as Duty

The conception of *wei-wu-wei* as a duty can be justified from the deontological, consequentialist and the perfectionist perspectives. It is a well-known fact that the concept of duty is directly concerned with the sense of *ought.* Let us try to understand these justifications one by one. In the deontological context, a duty is something that ought to be done without any considerations of motives or results. It ought to be performed just for the sake of it, without any personal considerations. The concept of *wei-wu-wei* has *hsu* as its associated precondition, which requires the abandonment of all personal considerations altogether. *Wei-wu-wei* ought to be performed because it is inherently in harmony with the universal reality and nature itself. Since *wei-wu-wei* springs from the inner spiritual nature, therefore it is inherently in harmony with the universal spiritual reality as well. There is no place for any personal consideration in determining the *oughtness* of *wei-wu-wei.* Thus, from the deontological perspective, *wei-wu-wei* emerges as a prime duty.

From the consequentialist perspective, it can be seen that the performance of *wei-wu-wei* naturally leads to the enhancement of peace and harmony in the world. It also relieves one from the misery and frustration associated with the failure of an action. By performing *wei-wu-wei,* one moves closer to the self and the Tao. This immediately leads to greater sense of peace and harmony within oneself, as also with the world at large. The consequences of the continuous performance of *wei-wu-wei* are thus beneficial for both the self as well as the world. It is capable of eradicating strife and misery from the world, if adopted by one and all. Thus, *wei-wu-wei* has both phenomenal and spiritual beneficial consequences. Therefore, the adoption of *wei-wu-wei* may be easily justified as a duty, as an *ought,* for the betterment of the self as well as the world.

When we look at *wei-wu-wei* from the perspective of perfectionism, then we have to take note of the fact that the most basic and transcendent reality, that serves as the origin of everything, must be the most perfect as well. That is, the farther away one is from the Tao, the more imperfect would be that person. Now, *wei-wu-wei* has the inherent capability of removing worldliness and egoism from one's mind. It is the covering of worldliness and egoism over one's mind that keeps one away from realizing the nature of the omnipresent Tao. Therefore, if one is interested in realizing the highest perfection, then the continuous and diligent practice of *wei-wu-wei* must be taken as a basic duty. The practice of *wei-wu-wei* gradually removes the covering over the nature of Tao and once that cover is completely removed, Tao manifests in its purity and perfection. Such pure manifestation of the Tao within oneself intuitively reveals its nature to that person. As a result of this manifestation, that person comes in perfect harmony with the Tao, and since Tao is the most perfect, that person also acquires the highest possible perfection in his thoughts, words and actions. Thus, the unrelenting practice of *wei-wu-wei* leads one to the highest perfection. Therefore, from the perfectionist viewpoint as well, *wei-wu-wei* emerges as a prime *ought* or duty. Thus, from various possible ethical perspectives, the continuous practice of *wei-wu-wei* emerges as a prime duty for one and all.

Chapter 6:
Universal Value and Unfailing Nature of Spiritual Duty

The very concept of spiritual duty has a necessary reference and relation to some spiritual framework, where the term 'Spiritual', deriving from the term 'spirit', again necessarily points towards some non-material principle or ideal. What should our duties be? What *ought* to be done? This is the most important question of ethics and related with this is the question why we *ought* to do something. These questions have been answered from various perspectives, depending on the theoretical stance taken by the thinker. It may be answered from the deontological perspective or the consequentialist perspective or the perfectionist perspective or the intuitionist perspective or possibly even some other perspective. Duty in the context of these different perspectives has already been elaborately discussed in the first chapter. The fourth and fifth chapters have discussed the concept of duty in the context of the niṣkāma-karma of Bhagavadgītā and *wei-wu-wei* of Taoism.

One important point needs to be noted about the previous discussions. All the theoretical perspectives discussed in the first chapter do not essentially have a spiritual framework associated with them. On the contrary, the discussions of duty in the context of Bhagavadgītā and Taoism essentially have a spiritual framework associated with them. But what is the significance of this distinction? That is to say, is there any significant difference between the conception of duty in the spiritual and non-spiritual frameworks? More specifically, can the concept of *ought* be related to or even derived from the positivist metaphysical conception of reality? These are just some of the questions to which the responses of contemporary ethical thinkers and the traditional spiritual traditions widely differ. Therefore, it is pertinent to critically evaluate these differences and their acclaimed justifications. This chapter seeks to go into this critical evaluation for the sake of a better understanding of the concept of duty in different kinds of frameworks.

6.1 Comparison of Niṣkāma-karma and Wei-wu-wei in the Context of Duty

Bhagavadgītā presents the concept of niṣkāma-karma as the core of karma-yoga, which is one of the three important paths to union with the higher spiritual reality. Thus, it has been essentially presented in a spiritual metaphysical framework. The ultimate objective and result of the perfect practice of niṣkāma-karma is presented to have the highest possible spiritual value, namely perfect union with God or Brahman. But what is niṣkāma-karma? Basically speaking, it is the performance of one's duties and obligations, with perfect detachment to its anticipated results or fruits. But what are the presuppositions of the perfect practice of niṣkāma-karma? Certainly, it is not the common way of performing any action. Usually, one undertakes an action for the sake of its anticipated results. Even when a person performs an action, taking it as his duty, there is often a consideration of the possible outcomes of the performance and non-performance of that duty for the self as well as the world. In the context of the contemporary ethical theories, the consideration of these outcomes is restricted to the mundane or phenomenal sphere. But, in the case of niṣkāma-karma, the most significant consequences of its performance or non-performance are clearly spiritual in nature and transcend the mundane sphere and also the present physical life. This has far reaching implications. Let us take a look at some of the important features of niṣkāma-karma, in the context of duty.

1. The practice of niṣkāma-karma requires detachment from the anticipated results of the actions performed as one's duties. Such detachment requires an even minded indifference to the pleasant and unpleasant results of those actions. This in turn requires an indifference to the reactions of the body and mind to the possible pleasant and unpleasant experiences. Such mental and physical indifference to various kinds of experiences, thus becomes a precondition for the proper practice of niṣkāma-karma.

2. The requirement of mental and physical indifference works against the common inbuilt conviction of identification with our physical bodies. The conviction of bodily identification is the most basic form of spiritual ignorance and bondage in the spiritual framework of Bhagavadgītā. Hence, the practice of mental and physical indifference strikes at the very root of spiritual ignorance and bondage.

3. Thus, the practice of niṣkāma-karma subtly works as an effective spiritual discipline, having the capacity to completely eradicate the very root of spiritual ignorance and bondage. Therefore, the perfection of niṣkāma-karma has the potential to grant the highest spiritual knowledge and liberation.

4. The practice of niṣkāma-karma does not explicitly require the acceptance of any religious or spiritual

metaphysical category. It can be perfectly practised even by an atheist. Thus, the practice of niṣkāma-karma does not essentially have any religious or spiritual attachments associated with it.

5. Since the practice of niṣkāma-karma requires the performance of only one's duties and obligations, therefore all actions motivated by selfish considerations of attachment and aversion, happiness and misery, pleasure and pain, etc. have to be shunned. Thus, all selfish actions have to be given up.

6. The duties to be performed under the practice of niṣkāma-karma are decided by one's status and position in life, society and the state, as well as by the person's intrinsic dispositions. Thus, the activities performed under niṣkāma-karma are inherently designed to cater to the requirements and wellbeing of the family, society, state and the world.

7. Thus, the activities of niṣkāma-karma are designed to promote the common good of the family, society, state and the world. Thus, niṣkāma-karma is designed to enhance the common good, at the phenomenal plane.

8. The concept of *yajña* in the Vedic tradition is primarily that of recognizing and reinforcing the various natural forces and resources, which is thus inherently designed to promote the good of all. Therefore, the practice of niṣkāma-karma too may be treated as a *yajña* in the Vedic sense, because it effectively enhances the common good, through the detached performance of various duties.

9. The concept of *loka-saṅgraha* in the Bhagavadgītā refers to the promotion of the common welfare. The unselfish promotion of the common good, practiced in a detached manner, as a matter of duty, is called *loka-saṅgraha.* All

phenomenal duties and obligations are primarily aimed at the promotion of the common good, therefore, the activities performed as niṣkāma-karma automatically aim at the promotion of *loka-saṅgraha.* Thus, niṣkāma-karma is inherently designed to promote *loka-saṅgraha.*

10. The practice of niṣkāma-karma cannot be perfect all of a sudden. It has to be practised diligently and continuously, even though it will be imperfect in the initial stages. In fact, the degree of imperfection of its practice goes on decreasing gradually, until it becomes completely perfect. The culminating perfection of niṣkāma-karma implies the highest spiritual knowledge and liberation.

11. Thus, the practice and perfection of niṣkāma-karma naturally leads to spiritual enlightenment, even though one may not be having any religious or spiritual faith and conviction while practising niṣkāma-karma.

12. The practice of niṣkāma-karma is inherently capable of ensuring both the phenomenal good as well as spiritual enlightenment and liberation. It ensures the highest good for both the self as well as the world.

13. The practice of niṣkāma-karma and karma-yoga restrains one from lapsing into passivity and inactivity. It declares that even after one has perfected niṣkāma-karma and become a *sthitaprajña,* he needs to be continuously engaged in his duties in a detached manner for the promotion of common good and for setting up an ideal example for the masses.

Now, let us take a look at the characteristic features of the *wei-wu-wei* of Taoism.

1. The concept of *wei-wu-wei* is that of action in non-action. Non-action here refers to the negation of worldly

actions, which are characterized by their selfish motivations related to attachment and aversion, pleasure and pain, etc. Thus, non-action stands for the negation of worldly actions, which are characterized by worldly desires. *Wei-wu-wei* or action in non-action, therefore, refers to those actions which are not prompted by worldly desires and selfish motivations.

2. The performance of *wei-wu-wei* therefore requires the emptying of the mind of all worldly desires and selfish motivations or *hsu*. This requires the suppression and eradication of one's ego, as well as the eradication of the conviction of bodily identification.

3. Such requirement of the eradication of one's ego and sense of bodily identification effectively makes the practice of *wei-wu-wei* a spiritual discipline.

4. What sort of actions would come under the purview of *wei-wu-wei*? Certainly, all selfish and desire motivated actions would be ruled out. Taoism does not accept or prescribe even the duties prescribed by the worldly people. It prescribes following the way of the Tao, which means following the ways of nature.

5. What does following the way of Tao mean in Taoism? It means acting in accordance with the most fundamental law of nature i.e. the law of reversion or *fan*. This law chalks out a course of actions and changes for each entity in the world and acting in accordance with that plan is following the way of Tao.

6. Such a natural course of action is prompted by our inner being or consciousness, if we free our minds from all worldly desires and ego. Further, imbibing the characteristics of the Tao is also treated as following the way of Tao. Humility,

gentleness, simplicity, desire lessness, spontaneity etc. are some of the inherent characteristics of the Tao. Therefore, the cultivation of these qualities in a natural manner too comes under the purview of *wei-wu-wei.*

7. The practice of *wei-wu-wei* presupposes *hsu* or emptiness of the mind of all worldly desires and ego. *Hsu* is itself to be cultivated through the practice of silence, solitude and withdrawal from the worldly environment.

8. Tao ensures universal harmony and spiritual growth of all the entities in the world. Tao manifests itself as the law of reversion in the phenomenal world. Therefore, following the ways and characteristics of the Tao promotes peace and harmony, as well as spiritual growth of one and all.

9. The practice of *wei-wu-wei* cannot be perfect all of a sudden. Its practice by the spiritual aspirant requires emptiness or *hsu,* which can be cultivated only gradually through continuous efforts. Nonetheless, the continuous effort and practice leads to gradual improvement, which culminates in the perfection of both *hsu* as well as *wei-wu-wei.*

10.Strictly speaking, the practice and perfection of *wei-wu-wei* requires only *hsu* or the emptiness of the mind of all worldly desires and ego. It does not require faith in any transcendent spiritual category. As such, it can be practiced even by an atheist.

11.Although *wei-wu-wei* can be practiced without having any spiritual faith and conviction, yet its perfection naturally reveals the transcendent nature, absoluteness and universal immanence of the Tao, which amounts to spiritual enlightenment.

12. The concept of duty is negative in Taoism. One *ought* to get rid of all selfishness and worldly desires through continuous diligent efforts. Gradual success in this effort naturally leads one to the way of the Tao.

13. The perfection of *wei-wu-wei* causes the Tao realized master to act spontaneously in accordance with the promptings of his inner nature or consciousness. Natural spontaneity is the characteristic of spiritual masters.

14. The acts of *wei-wu-wei* necessarily illustrate humility, which is treated as the highest virtue in Taoism. Thus, *wei-wu-wei* is highly effective in ensuring peace and harmony in the world. Thus, *wei-wu-wei* may be considered as a categorical *ought* and duty, keeping in view both its phenomenal and spiritual potential and values.

Keeping in view the salient features of niṣkāma-karma and *wei-wu-wei,* as outlined above, we can easily see that there are many points of similarity between them, but there are also some important points of difference as well. Let us first take a look at their similarities.

1. Both niṣkāma-karma and *wei-wu-wei* are central concepts of great spiritual traditions. The metaphysical frameworks of both Bhagavadgītā and Taoism are spiritual and absolutist in their natures. Both the higher aspect of Brahman and the higher Tao are transcendent and absolute ontological realities. Both of them are beyond the reach of space, time, causality, reason and language.

2. Both niṣkāma-karma and *wei-wu-wei* have two aspects each. The first aspect is that when they are practiced as spiritual disciplines for the sake of realizing the highest spiritual reality. This is their aspect of spiritual discipline. The

second aspect is that when they become the natural characteristics of a sage having the realization of the highest spiritual reality. The aspect of spiritual discipline requires great effort and mental control, whereas the aspect of spiritual perfection becomes perfectly effortless and natural for the realized sage.

3. The practice of niṣkāma-karma and *wei-wu-wei* as spiritual disciplines remains imperfect, even though their continuous practice goes on reducing the imperfection. Similarly, as the characteristics of spiritual realization, both of them are necessarily perfect.

4. Although both niṣkāma-karma and *wei-wu-wei* are the central disciplines of spiritual traditions, yet the practice of both of them does not necessarily require faith or conviction in transcendent spiritual matters. Both of them may be practiced even by atheists in a successful manner.

5. The effective practice of both niṣkāma-karma and *wei-wu-wei* requires becoming indifferent to the bodily and mental experiences of pleasure and pain, happiness and misery, honour and dishonour, heat and cold, etc.

6. The practice of both niṣkāma-karma and *wei-wu-wei* requires refraining from acting on the basis of selfish motivations. Actions done on the basis of egoistic considerations cannot be treated as niṣkāma-karma or *wei-wu-wei*.

7. Both niṣkāma-karma and *wei-wu-wei* are not performed for the sake of enjoying the anticipated results of those actions. Both presuppose detachment from the anticipated results of the actions undertaken.

8. The practice of both niṣkāma-karma and *wei-wu-wei* weakens the conviction of bodily identification. Their practice strikes at the most basic form of spiritual ignorance.

9. The practice of both of them enhances peace and harmony in the world. Their practice elevates the level of the common good. That is, their practice leads to greater good and welfare of all at the phenomenal plane.

10. The practice and perfection of both niṣkāma-karma and *wei-wu-wei* lead to spiritual upliftment and realization. They lead to the intuitive realization of the transcendent and absolute Brahman and the Tao.

11. The practice of both niṣkāma-karma and *wei-wu-wei* are treated as a basic *ought* or duty, irrespective of all motivations and objectives.

12. Both of them illustrate the case of non-worldly actions. They are the examples of spiritual actions, rooted in the spiritual nature of the self and the higher reality. Both of them are, therefore, cases of external actions but internal non-actions. Hence, instead of binding the agent of that action, they actually uplift him spiritually.

13. The practice of both of them destroys the worldly ego and inculcates humility, the highest spiritual virtue. The perfection of both of them leads to the intuitive realization and conviction of one's basic identity with everything in the world. At the same time, their perfection also gives the conviction of one's ontological transcendence and immutability. That is, the perfection of both of them leads to the intuitive realization and conviction of one's universal phenomenal immanence and ontological transcendence and immutability.

Let us now take a look at the points of difference between niṣkāma-karma and *wei-wu-wei.*

1. The concept of niṣkāma-karma advocates the detached performance of our duties and obligations, as prescribed by the scriptures, tradition and the state. On the other hand, the concept of *wei-wu-wei* advocates moving away from the worldly norms and values and instead insists on following the spontaneous promptings of our inner spiritual nature. These spontaneous inner promptings are believed to be in accordance with the universal law of reversion or *fan.*

2. In the case of niṣkāma-karma, stress is laid upon being totally detached from the anticipated results of the performed action. But in the case of *wei-wu-wei,* stress is laid upon the emptiness of the mind from all worldly desires and ego, which is called *hsu.* The degree of this emptiness directly determines the degree of perfection of *wei-wu-wei.*

3. In the case of niṣkāma-karma, the *guṇas* are considered to be the real agents of actions, whereas in the case of *wei-wu-wei,* the Tao itself is considered the real agent of all actions.

4. In the case of perfection of niṣkāma-karma, the *sthitaprajña* person is supposed to willingly go on performing his duties for the sake of common good and setting the right example. But, in the case of perfection of *wei-wu-wei,* the Tao realized sage follows only the spontaneous promptings of his inner spiritual nature.

5. The practice and perfection of niṣkāma-karma explicitly aims for the promotion of the common good, variously referred to as *yajña* and *loka-saṅgraha.* But the practice and perfection of *wei-wu-wei* does not explicitly aim

for the promotion of the common good, even though indirectly it too effects the promotion of the common good.

6.2 Concept of Duty in Spiritual and Non-spiritual Frameworks

The concept of duty is necessarily related with the concept of *ought*. Duty is a normative concept and there is an inherent sense of obligation attached with it. But there are various approaches to understand the different aspects related with the concept of this *ought*. For example, the contextual and conceptual circumstances associated with this sense of *ought* may be explained in various ways, which leads to different ethical theories. Here, we are interested in approaching the issue from the perspective of spiritual and non-spiritual frameworks. But, first let us be clear about what we mean by a spiritual framework. Broadly speaking, a spiritual framework refers to the metaphysical and conceptual framework in which the most fundamental nature of the self as well as that of everything else is some sort of an immaterial conscious reality. On the other hand, a non-spiritual framework would be that in which consciousness is not accepted as a separate immaterial ontological category.

Let us first try to comprehend the nature of duty in a non-spiritual framework. In such a framework, the basic ontological nature of all entities is taken to be material. There is no place for belief in the any kind of existence before one's physical birth and also after one's physical death. Hence, the concept of one's existence is strictly limited to the present physical life and that defines the total sphere of one's existence, activities and experiences. In this scenario, the notion of duty must also be completely restricted to and defined by the various factors related with the present physical life. There are various approaches to ethics and duty in the non-spiritual framework such as the deontological approach, the consequentialist approach, the utilitarian approach, the intuitionist approach, the perfectionist approach, etc.

Let us try to take a brief look at the characteristics and limitations of these various approaches to ethics and duty. In the deontological approach, duty *ought* to be performed for the sake of duty alone. Duty is presented as a categorical imperative. Now, human beings are thinking rational beings. It would be rather naïve to presume that they should or they would accept anything as a categorical imperative without being satisfied with some acceptable explanation and justification. Further, if any explanation is sought to be given in terms of its ultimate collective consequence, then it no longer remains a matter of categorical imperative. Thus, in both the alternative situations, the deontological approach falls short of the requirement of rational acceptability. In the case of the consequentialist approach, the *oughtness* of an action or duty is treated as a direct function of its consequences. That is, the consequences and results of an action are critical in deciding the desirability of an action as a duty. Here the problem is that the actual result of any given action is always the net outcome of many impinging factors, over which the agent of the action has little or no control. Therefore, the actual result of the same action may be quite different in different situations. But if the results keep on varying for the same action, then how can its desirability as a duty be decided according to the consequentialist approach! As per the consequentialist approach something may be decided as a duty only on the grounds of the desirability of its consequences, but if the consequences of that action are variable, then its determination as a duty would be unjustified. So, the determination of an action as a duty becomes quite indefinite in the consequentialist approach to ethics. The utilitarian approach to ethics and duty too is dogged by the same kind of objections. In this approach, the utility of the results of an action is critical for determining its acceptance as a duty. But the concept of utility is a relative concept and it must be with respect to some person or group of persons. It is a well-known fact that almost every person is unique in his ordering of preferential utilities. So, what may be of great utility to one person, may not have the same kind of utility for another person. In this scenario, making the utility of the result of an action the critical criterion for the determination of a duty, turns out to be highly objectionable. When we take a look at the intuitionist approach to ethics and duty in a non-spiritual framework, it has to be conceded that the critical importance here is to be attached to the sense of intuition. Now, intuition may be understood as a cognitive faculty which is trans-rational in nature. Even then, it cannot be denied in a non-spiritual framework that all the sense experiences and mental activities of a person mould the shape of all cognitive faculties. Further, the sense experiences and mental activities of all persons are unique in their totality. Therefore, the moulding of all the cognitive faculties turns out to be unique for each and every person. This means the functional structure of the intuitive faculty would also be unique for each and every person. If so, it would be almost impossible to designate any action as a duty for all on the basis of individual intuitive cognitions suggesting that it be accepted as an *ought* or duty. Now, let us come to the perfectionist approach to ethics and duty. In this approach, an action is considered as a duty if it is accepted that it would lead to the perfection of the individual. This means the idea of perfection is critical for the determination of an action as a duty. However, the problem is that there is no universally acceptable notion of perfection. Each person has a different order of priorities and hence, a different notion of perfection. This means, what may be acceptable as a duty for one person, may not be so for another person. Thus, extreme subjectivity of perfection would render the whole objective of ethics impracticable. Thus, we have seen that the various possible approaches to ethics and duty in the non-spiritual framework fail to present a coherent and consistent conception of duty.

Now, let us take a look at the concept of duty in a spiritual framework. While considering the nature of duty in spiritual frameworks, we shall primarily refer to the Taoist framework and the framework of Bhagavadgītā. In these frameworks, there is a clear conception of moral and metaphysical perfection. There is a clear conception of the fundamental nature of all phenomenal entities, including the self, and it is believed to be universally common and spiritual in nature. It is believed to be transcendent to space, time, causality, reason and language. The phenomenal world of dualities, such as pleasure and pain, happiness and misery, life and death, honour and dishonour, heat and cold, etc. is considered to be only partially real. In contrast, the universal transcendent spiritual reality is believed to have the essential form of pure peace, harmony and bliss. It is considered to be ontologically immutable and incorruptible. Such a nature is believed to be the true nature of the self, as well as of everything else. In these spiritual frameworks, the non-realization of the true nature of ourselves and the world, is considered to be the source of all misery and dissatisfaction. This means, overcoming this basic spiritual ignorance and illusion must be considered imperative for the realization of true and lasting peace, bliss and harmony. This must be treated as the *ought* or categorical imperative of duty in the spiritual frameworks. All the spiritual disciplines prescribed in these spiritual frameworks are basically the various paths to the realization of this perfection. These spiritual disciplines are effective in removing the worldly covering lying over our basic ontological nature. The practice of niṣkāma-karma and *wei-wu-wei* has to be seen and appreciated in this light. It is interesting to note that the ethical approaches of deontology, consequentialism, utilitarianism, intuitionism and perfectionism, may all be applied in a more consistent and coherent manner in the spiritual frameworks, as compared to the non-spiritual frameworks. Taking an overall view of the spiritual framework, the duty of practicing the prescribed spiritual disciplines may be seen as a basic categorical imperative, which has a universally desirable consequence and an ultimate utility, which is prompted by our pure intuitive faculty and which leads to the realization of the highest possible perfection.

6.3 Relevance and Advantages of Concept of Duty in a Spiritual Framework

The characteristics of a spiritual framework, as well as the nature of duty in such a framework, have already been discussed in the previous sections. We have also done a comparison of the concept of duty in a spiritual framework and a non-spiritual framework. Now, we shall look into the relevance and advantages of the concept of duty in the context of a spiritual framework.

1. A spiritual framework talks of the ultimate reality beyond the realm of the phenomenal world. Its time horizon is also infinite, much beyond the limited span of the given physical life. The ultimate aim of the performance of duties too transcends the limitations of the given life time. All this has a serious implication for the concept and performance of duty in a spiritual framework. In such a framework, one would not be performing his duties with the mindset that the results and rewards of that performance would necessarily be coming along in the given life itself. One develops infinite patience, as a result of which he does not give up the performance of his duties, irrespective of the circumstances he may have to face. Such patience and diligence in the performance of one's duties is hard to find in the case of non-spiritual frameworks because there are explicit or implicit expectations of rewards for the performance of duties within the given life time. The inherent fragility of life makes the patient performance of duties even more difficult to sustain.

2. In a spiritual framework, great stress is laid explicitly or implicitly on giving up the conviction of one's identification with the physical body. It is treated as a part of one's duty. As a result of this discipline and practice, one develops the capacity to remain indifferent to the pleasant and unpleasant psycho-physical experiences. Thus, remaining indifferent to the various kinds of physical and mental experiences becomes a praiseworthy merit in the ethics of spiritual framework. As a result of this fortitude, the person remains always on the path of his duty. Such fortitude is difficult to develop in a non-spiritual framework.

3. The concept of duty in a spiritual framework highlights the importance of eradicating all selfish and egoistic ideas and

motivations. This immediately rules out all sorts of negative motivations for actions, making the world a better place to live in. Such eradication of negative ideas and motivations is rather difficult of achieve in non-spiritual frameworks.

4. All spiritual frameworks directly or indirectly talk of the universal immanence of the ultimate ontological reality. As a result of this, one gets convinced about one's fundamental identity with all entities in the world. Such conviction strongly inhibits selfishness and promotes the common good and welfare. Such natural unselfish promotion of the common good is extremely difficult to realize in a non-spiritual framework.

5. The performance of the prescribed duties does not necessarily require one to accept transcendental spiritual entities, in the case of a spiritual framework. That is, having faith in God or some similar higher reality is not a prerequisite for the proper performance of the prescribed spiritual duties. Even an atheist can sincerely practice the spiritual disciplines of niṣkāma-karma and *wei-wu-wei*.

6. In a spiritual framework, the perfection and culmination of the performance of prescribed duties lead one to have the intuitive realization of the self, which is by itself an indubitable proof for the categorical worthiness of following our duties. The realized masters vouch for the effectiveness and worthiness of the prescribed duties for attaining the intuitive realization of the self and its transcendent universal nature. This provides a solid foundation for the sincere practice of the prescribed duties in a spiritual framework. Such a solid motivational foundation for the performance of our duties is difficult to come across in a non-spiritual framework.

7. The prescribed duties in a spiritual framework are open for one and all and they can be easily practiced by anyone, irrespective of their place in society. No preconditions need to be fulfilled for their practice. It has the capacity to weed out all negativity from the world. All this rather difficult to find in a non-spiritual framework.

8. The practice of humility is a central duty in any spiritual framework. Its practice and perfection is destined to make the person and the world a better place to live in. But, in the non-spiritual frameworks, humility is seldom stressed upon. This makes a world of difference between the spiritual and non-spiritual frameworks of ethics and duty.

Bibliography

Primary Sources

1. Lao-Tse, Tr. Legge, James, *The Tao Teh King or The Tao and its Characteristics*, www.FreeSpiritualEbooks.com, 2008.
2. Lao Tzu, Tr. Kline, A. S., *Tao Te Ching: The Book of the Way and its Virtue*, Poetry in Translation, 2003.
3. *Śrīmadbhagavadgītā Śrīmadbhagavadgītā*, Gītā Press, Gorakhpur.
4. Bhave, Vinoba, *Talks on the Gītā*, Vinoba Sarva Seva Sangh Prakashan, Varanasi, 1970.
5. Aurobindo, *Gītā Prabandha (Part I)*, Shri Arvind Ashram, Pondicherry, 1955.
6. Aurobindo, *Gītā Prabandha (Part II)*, Shri Arvind Ashram, Pondicherry, 1959.
7. Tilak, Bal Gangadhar, *Śrīmadbhagavadgītā Rahasya*, T. J. Tilak and S. S. Tilak (Private Publication), Pune, 1984.
8. Radhakrishnan, S., *Bhagavadgītā*, Saraswati Vihar, 1989.
9. Gambhīrānanda, Swāmī, Tr., *Bhagavadgītā: with the commentary of Śaṅkarācārya*, Advaita Ashram, 2012.
10. Goyandka, Harikrishnadas, Tr., *Śrīmadbhagavadgītā (with Hindi translation of*

Śaṅkara's commentary), Gītā Press, Gorakhpur.

11. Aristotle, Tr. Reeve, C. D. C., *Nicomachean Ethics*, Hackett Publishing Company,

Cambridge, 2014.

Secondary Sources

1. Mishra, Yogish kumar, *Philosophical Religions of the World,* Koras Press Ltd., London, 2012.
2. Smart, Ninian, *World Philosophies,* Routledge Taylor & Francis Group, London, 2000.
3. Weber, Max, Tr. Ed. Gerth, Hans H., *The Religion of China: Confucianism and Taoism,* The Free Press of Glencoe, 1962.
4. Frankena, W. K., *Is morality logically dependent on religion,* Religion and Morality, Ed. G. Outka and J. P. Reeder, Anchor\Doubleday, New York, 1973.
5. Brody, B., *Morality and religion reconsidered in his Readings in the Philosophy of Religion: An analytic approach,* Prentice Hall, New Jersey, 1974.
6. Foot, Philippa, ed. *Theories of Ethics,* Oxford University Press, New York, 1990.
7. Ross, W. D., *Kant's Ethical Theory,* Oxford University Press, Oxford, 1954.
8. Singer, Peter, ed. *A Companion to Ethics,* Blackwell Publishers, Oxford, 1994.
9. Sidgwick, Henry, *Outlines of the History of Ethics,* Beacon Publishers, Boston, 1960.
10. Sidgwick, Henry, *The method of Ethics,* Dover Publishers, New York, 1974.
11. Macintyre, Alasdair, *After Virtue,* Duckworth Publishers, London, 1981.
12. Mackie, J. L., *Ethics: Inventing Right and Wrong,* Penguin Publishers, Harmondsworth, 1977.

13. Perry, Ralph Barton, *General Theory of Value,* Harvard University Press, Cambridge, 1954.
14. Ross, W. D., *The Right and Good,* Oxford University Press, Oxford, 1930.
15. Singer, Peter, *Ethics,* Oxford University Press, Oxford, 1994.
16. Frankena, William K., *Ethics,* Prentice Hall of India Pvt. Ltd., New Delhi, 1989.
17. Macintyre, Alasdair, *A Short History of Ethics,* London.
18. Sterba, James P., *Ethics: The Big Question,* Wiley Blackwell, 2009.
19. Saroja, G. V., *Tilak and Śankara on Bhagavadgītā,* Sterling Publishers, New Delhi, 1985.
20. Besant, Annie and Das, Bhagvān, *The Bhagavadgītā,* Radha Publications, New Delhi, 1993.
21. Fung, Yu-Lan, *A Short History of Chinese Philosophy,* Tr. D. Bodde, The Macmillan Company, New York, 1958.
22. Graham, A., *Chuang-Tzu: The Inner Chapters,* George Allen & Unwin, London, 1981.
23. Smullyan, R., *The Tao is Silent,* Harper & Row, New York, 1977.
24. Edwards, Paul, *The Encyclopedia pf Philosophy,* vol. 2, The Macmillan Company, New York, 1967.
25. Schuhmacher, Stephan and Woerner, Gest, ed. *The Rider Encyclopedia of Eastern Philosophy and Religion,* London, 1989.

26. Borchart, Donald M., ed. *Borchart Encyclopedia of Philosophy,* vol. 2, Thomson Gale Publisher, 2006.

27. Magill, Frank N., ed. *Masterpieces of World Philosophy,* Harper & Row Publishers, New York, 1961.

28. Bowker, John, ed. *The Oxford Dictionary of World Religion,* Oxford University Press, Oxford, 1997.

29. Bettany, G. T., *Encyclopedia of World Religion,* Bracken Books, London, 1990.

30. Gwinn, Robert P., ed. *The New Encyclopedia Britannica,* vol. 2, 1985.

31. Smith, Huston, *Religion of Man,* Harper & Row Publisher, New York, 1958.

32. Eliade, Mircea, ed. *The Encyclopedia of Religion,* vol. 14, Macmillan Publishing Company, New York, 1987.

33. Hastings, James, ed. *Encyclopedia of Religion and Ethics,* vol. 12, Charles Scribner's Sons, New York, 1961.

34. Jurji, Edward J., ed. *The Great Religions of the Modern World,* Princeton University Press, Princeton, 1967.

35. Noss, David S., *A History of the World's Religions,* Prentice Hall, New Jersey, 1999.

36. Das, Bhagavan, *The Essential Unity of all Religions,* Kashi Vidyapeeth, Varanasi, 1994.

37. McCasland, S. Vernon, *Religions of the World,* Random House, New York, 1969.

38. Eastman, Roger, ed. *The Ways of Religion: An Introduction to the Major Traditions,* Oxford University Press, Oxford, 1993.

39. Dye, James W., *Religions of the World,* Appleton Century Crafts, New York, 1967.

40. Gardner, James, *Encyclopedia of Faiths and Religions of the World,* Aryan Books International, New Delhi, 1999.

41. Brandon, S. G. F., *A Dictionary of Comparative Religion,* Weidenfeld &Nicolson, London, 1970.

42. Lillie, William, *An Introduction to Ethics,* Allied Publishers Pvt. Ltd., New Delhi, 1967.

43. Sharma, C. D., *A Critical Survey of Indian Philosophy,* MLBD, New Delhi, 1991.

JOURNALS

1. Swinburne, R. G., *Duty and the Will of God,* Canadian Journal of Philosoph